www.wadsworth.com

www.wadsworth.com is the World Wide Web site for Thomson Wadsworth and is your direct source to dozens of online resources.

At *www.wadsworth.com* you can find out about supplements, demonstration software, and student resources. You can also send e-mail to many of our authors and preview new publications and exciting new technologies.

www.wadsworth.com
Changing the way the world learns®

LENSES ON TEACHING

Developing Perspectives on Classroom Life

Fourth Edition

Leigh Chiarelott
Bowling Green State University

Leonard Davidman
California Polytechnic State University,
San Luis Obispo

Kevin Ryan
Boston University

THOMSON
™
WADSWORTH

Australia • Brazil • Canada • Mexico • Singapore • Spain • United Kingdom • United States

THOMSON

WADSWORTH

Lenses on Teaching: Developing Perspectives on Classroom Life, **Fourth Edition**
Leigh Chiarelott, Leonard Davidman, and Kevin Ryan

Publisher/Executive Editor: *Vicki Knight*
Education Editor: *Dan Alpert*
Development Editor: *Tangelique Williams*
Editorial Assistant: *Ann Richards*
Marketing Manager: *Terra Schultz*
Marketing Assistant: *Rebecca Weisman*
Marketing Communications Manager: *Tami Strang*
Project Manager, Editorial Production: *Emily Smith*
Creative Director: *Rob Hugel*
Art Director: *Maria Epes*

Print Buyer: *Linda Hsu*
Permissions Editor: *Roberta Broyer*
Production Service: *Interactive Composition Corporation*
Copy Editor: *Meg McDonald*
Cover Designer: *Liz Harasymczuk*
Cover Image: *Todd Davidson/Illustration Works/Getty Images*
Compositor: *Interactive Composition Corporation*
Text and Cover Printer: *West Group*

Library of Congress Control Number: 2005937610

ISBN 0-495-09190-1

Thomson Higher Education
10 Davis Drive
Belmont, CA 94002-3098
USA

For more information about our products, contact us at:
Thomson Learning Academic Resource Center
1-800-423-0563

For permission to use material from this text or product, submit a request online at
http://www.thomsonrights.com.
Any additional questions about permissions can be submitted by e-mail to
thomsonrights@thomson.com.

This book is dedicated to the classroom teachers who inspired us and who will inspire the next generation of teachers.

Brief Contents

CONTENTS

PREFACE

In recent years, national attention has been focused upon how best to prepare teachers for the twenty-first century. When, how, and where teachers should be educated have been hotly debated by national commissions, teachers' organizations, and teacher education institutions. One of the common threads through all these proposals for change has been the need for teacher candidates to observe and participate in schools and classrooms early and often in their preparation programs. However, in these early field experiences, quantity of observations can easily be confused with quality of experiences. To the untrained eye, one classroom practice could appear as effective as another. *Having* an experience is not, as John Dewey noted, the same as *learning* from an experience. The potential for an experience to be non- or mis-educative is increased anytime that experience is not accompanied by reflection, analysis, and summation of what has been learned from the reflective process.

Because teacher education is a constantly changing professional field, the experiences teacher candidates have today are quite different from those they might have experienced fifteen years ago or even five years ago. The fourth edition of *Lenses on Teaching* addresses a number of these changes. Among these changes are:

- a new chapter on contemporary issues affecting teachers' decision-making and their daily practice, such as No Child Left Behind and school violence;
- increased attention to the teacher as a reflective practitioner;
- updated discussions of research and practice on teaching students with special needs, teaching in diverse settings, and the utilization of technology to facilitate learning;
- new material on standards for teachers and national assessment of teaching such as Praxis and Pathwise;
- redesigned activities on ethical decision-making and learning about the community in which you will teach;
- updated examples of how media models affect the image of teachers;
- updated and redesigned Core and Suggested Activities throughout the book.

We hope that these changes will provide reflective, analytical learning experiences for teacher candidates as they become more discriminating observers of schools and the process of schooling. As a teacher candidate, you are beginning a journey that will help you acquire concepts, skills, and dispositions that research suggests will help you develop into effective teachers. It is a long journey that will last your entire career. We trust that *Lenses on Teaching* will contribute to your understanding of both the journey and what you will encounter along the way.

We have developed this text as a guidebook to help you perceive and understand the many things that you'll see and do in pre-K-12 classrooms in the next few weeks. You and your instructor may find it useful to do all of the activities in the chapters, or you may find it necessary to only do the Core Activity in each chapter. How little or how much you do will be dependent upon your background experience and knowledge and your desire to derive as much benefit as possible from the field experience in which you're placed. In either case, we trust that your experience will be educative.

Although the content of this workbook is ultimately the responsibility of the authors, many persons have contributed in various ways to its successful production. To the many preservice candidates, graduate assistants, and classroom teachers who have shared their conceptual lenses with us and inspired our work through their visions of teaching, we are deeply indebted. To the reviewers whose critiques and insightful suggestions made the text more readable and the activities more workable, we are especially grateful. This group of reviewers include: John J. Chiodo, University of Oklahoma; Bill K. Gaedke, Jr., Eastern New Mexico University; Leanna Manna, Villa Maria College; Edie L. Norlin, Ohio State University; and Rhonda Westerhaus, Pratt Community College.

In addition to those who helped inspire and/or enhance the content of the textbook, we also wish to thank those who contributed to the production of the fourth edition of *Lenses on Teaching*. The Word Processing Center in the College of Education and Human Development at Bowling Green State University was an immensely valuable resource in the timely and efficient production of the original draft. Special thanks go to Judy Maxey for her exceptional work in typing the revisions and submitting them to the copy editor, Anupam Mukherjee, and Karel Floyd at California Polytechnic University, San Luis Obispo, who did all of the typing for the drafts of Chapters 4, 5, and 10. The authors gratefully acknowledge the work done by our graduate research assistants, Katie Lariccia and Melissa Meiers. Their timely and in depth review of research materials related to the revisions were invaluable in preparing the manuscript. Of course, the fourth edition would not have been possible without the outstanding efforts of the editorial and production staffs at Thomson/Wadsworth, and we appreciate their support and expertise in making our vision a reality.

Finally, we are eternally grateful to our families and especially to our wives, Donna Chiarelott, Pat Davidman, and Marilyn Ryan who have supported our work on this textbook for the past 20 years. Without their encouragement and help this project would never have succeeded.

Chapter 1

INTRODUCTION TO *LENSES ON TEACHING*

Many of you are about to embark on a journey back to an environment where you spent a large portion of your childhood and youth. This time, however, you will be asked to look at this environment from a different perspective (or perhaps from multiple perspectives) than you did as a child. You will be looking at schools from these different perspectives to help you in your decision to become a teacher. Although you may have already made up your mind to become a teacher, you may be less certain about where you want to teach, what grade level or subject matter you will feel most confident working with, what type of learners you will find most challenging and rewarding to teach, what kind of school philosophy best mirrors your philosophy of teaching, and so forth. Part of the purpose of this journey is to enable you to explore these questions early in your teacher preparation program so you can not only decide whether you want to become a teacher, but also discover what kind of teacher you would like to become.

Over the past few decades, research on effective teaching and classroom management, and the role of field experiences in preparing teachers, has burgeoned. On the whole, this research supports the existence of effective teaching and classroom management techniques and has placed field experiences in a pivotal position in the attainment of these competencies.

Early in your field observations you will no doubt feel compelled to note useful techniques employed by the teachers you observe. Somewhat unconsciously, you will find yourself drawn to behaviors that seem to quiet down the students, encourage them to work, motivate interesting discussions, and even make students laugh. These "tricks," as they may seem to you, have an almost mystical effect in the hands of an artistic teacher, and there will be a natural tendency to try to mirror those behaviors. Unfortunately, less effective teachers often have "tricks" as well, and these may, at times, seem equally effective in terms of creating quiet, encouragement, motivation, and even enjoyment. Differentiating between the deep structure of classroom life and cosmetic changes brought on by "trickery" will be one of the major challenges facing you in field experiences. Knowing the important elements in field observation is a sign of developing maturity as a beginning teacher.

Helping you develop as a teacher is the purpose of this resource manual. In a structured, progressive manner, you will develop skills and knowledge as an insightful, effective observer of classrooms. You will learn to identify and analyze characteristics of schools, classrooms, and learners. You will identify teacher behaviors, both effective and ineffective, in a systematic, objective manner. You will use observation instruments that will introduce you to a language for describing classrooms. You will encounter new ideas about schools and schooling and create an "ideal" classroom. And you will learn strategies that will move you beyond objective, fragmented descriptions toward impressionistic, vivid, rich descriptions. All of these activities, through diverse means, will contribute to your development as a teacher.

To help you gain the skills to see clearly what is going on in schools and classrooms, you will complete a number of observational tasks. Each task is related to a key educational area. Embedded in the task are the major objectives to be attained in your field-based observations. Through a series of sequentially organized activities, you will see and understand much more of what is going on around you.

CENTRAL QUESTIONS

This chapter will give you an overview of the text as well as an understanding of the activities that we recommend you carry out in the field experience component of your teacher education program. Here we have posed some central questions that have shaped the content and form of this resource text. These questions and our responses to them will help you use this resource text more effectively.

QUESTION 1: WHEN SHOULD STUDENTS ENGAGE IN FIELD OBSERVATIONS?

The recent past has seen a dramatic change in how teachers are prepared in the United States. Until the mid-1980s, most undergraduates preparing to be teachers took all of their general education and professional education courses on the college campus until their senior year. At that point they were sent out to student teach in an elementary or secondary school. There were many problems with that approach. First, some students had to wait for three or four years to discover that although they liked certain things about education and the teaching career, they were simply not suited for it. Second, the courses tended to be abstract and remote from the real world of children and schools. Third, the teachers-in-training had only their own experience as former elementary and secondary students on which to build. This sometimes caused trouble when their student teaching assignments were in different kinds of schools than they had gone through.

In recent years teacher training institutions all over the country have switched to programs that allow more and earlier observation of schools and communities prior to student teaching. Future teachers are sent into the field *during* their preparation, not at the end. The course for which you are using this text is part of the movement to offering earlier field observations and providing greater relevance to your training. Given this shift in perspective regarding the role of field experiences in teacher preparation, most teacher preparation programs emphasize that teacher candidates should participate in meaningful, systematic observations early in their teacher education programs.

QUESTION 2: HOW SHOULD THESE EXPERIENCES BE ORGANIZED TO ENSURE MEANINGFUL OBSERVATIONS?

A sequentially organized and varied set of field experiences should be a key component to this introductory course. Members of the teaching profession today—teachers, administrators, professors—believe that much of the content that you need to learn exists *within* schools and *within* classrooms and *within* the minds and hearts of the educational professionals with whom you will work. Initially you will observe the class-room and school using measurement instruments that require you simply to record information. These instruments will ask you to pay close attention to classroom be-haviors and to track them for short periods using specially designed coding systems. These instruments will *not* ask you to make judgments or to relate your knowledge and experiences about schools and schooling to the observations that you make. Later, as you become more familiar with descriptive ways of looking at classrooms, you will be asked to draw more inferences (i.e., make judgments) about what you are observ-ing. Ultimately you will be creating your "ideal vision" of classroom teaching as you see it and understand it.

QUESTION 3: **BESIDES OBSERVING CLASSROOM BEHAVIORS, WHAT MIGHT BE SOME OTHER VALUABLE RESOURCES FROM WHICH TO GATHER INFORMATION?**

You will begin as a classroom observer, carefully noting and recording what is going on around you. The technical name is *participant observer*. You will be a part of a classroom community with the teacher and students, but you will also be expected to observe what is going on around you. As you become more adept at participant obser-vation and more comfortable in your role as a describer of classroom interaction, you'll find that your perspectives are rather limited due to the narrow band of activities that you can observe and record. One technique that is particularly helpful in allowing us to see more with greater depth is interviewing. Although interviewing is a more com-plex and intrusive skill than observing, after you separate useful from inappropriate informants, the range of information made available will be of immeasurable value. Among the informants whom you will have the opportunity to interview are students, teachers, administrators, parents, and members of the school's community. The settings for these potential interviews include the classroom, teachers' lounge, school cafeteria, playground, school offices, school board meetings, and places of business in the com-munity. Perhaps, either in person or via e-mail, you will be able to visit the homes of students or teachers. No doubt you will find these various perspectives on schools, schooling, teachers, and teaching quite illuminating, although sometimes discouraging.

QUESTION 4: **HOW WILL THESE ACTIVITIES IN OBSERVING AND INTERVIEWING BE GUIDED?**

Early activities will have specific instructional objectives. By successfully completing an activity, you will attain the intended outcome of the learning experience. Subse-quent experiences will be equally well defined, but the outcomes may be oriented more toward problem solving or discovery. One purpose of these activities is to make you rely more on your own judgments so that you will begin to see yourself as an ef-fective decision maker.

QUESTION 5: **HOW MUCH OF THIS UNDERSTANDING OF SCHOOLS AND TEACHING WILL INVOLVE SELF-ANALYSIS ACTIVITIES?**

Prospective teachers in an introductory, field-based course should engage in self-analysis activities throughout the course to discern and describe the changes in their educational assumptions, the growth of their educational philosophy, and their personal desires and commitments toward teaching. We believe that while teaching requires certain skills and competencies, good teaching requires artistry. Inasmuch as artistry involves the projection of one's *self* onto or into a medium, artistic teaching is similarly a projection of one's *self* onto or into a classroom or electronic medium such as a home page on the Internet.

Artists frequently draw on their past experiences and use perceptions of these experiences as dominant themes in their art. As a teacher, you will also need to envision and clarify your experiences in learning and teaching with yourself and others and determine how they affect your perception of teaching. Teaching style is an extension of the teacher's experiences and personality—his or her expectations, goals, values, attitudes, dreams, and idiosyncrasies. In an effort to comprehend your emerging teaching style, you must, of necessity, come to grips with your *self*. An important part of teacher education is the recognition that you don't suddenly become a teacher at the conclusion of four or five years of preparation. You are becoming a teacher now, and you will continue to become a teacher throughout your professional career.

QUESTION 6: IN WHAT WAYS MIGHT THIS CONTINUOUS GROWTH BE FOSTERED?

Because of our belief in the importance of the growth process of teachers, we include a series of activities in the final chapter of this resource text. These self-education materials are designed to expand upon the observation and interviewing techniques that you have acquired and to supplement the self-analysis activities in which you have engaged.

This conception of continuous growth and the activities that support it are predicated upon the assumption that American schools have a critical need for effective teachers. Although the much-discussed teacher shortage (especially in math and science) that has recently captured national attention is reminiscent of a similar problem faced in the 1960s and 1980s, there is a key difference. Unfortunately, at that time emphasis was placed on educating *more* teachers to meet critical needs, and research on effective teaching had not yet progressed to the point that it could inform the burgeoning teacher education programs of the need for continuous growth experiences. In this first decade of our new century, we are in a much stronger position to design activities that support the continuing professional development of effective teachers.

QUESTION 7: WHAT IDEAS AND FACTS ABOUT TEACHING AND LEARNING INFORM OUR VISION OF "EFFECTIVE TEACHING" AND OUR SELECTION OF MEANINGFUL ACTIVITIES FOR INDIVIDUALS SEEKING TO BECOME TEACHERS?

In the past, educators had a somewhat narrow view of learning and teaching. Information was presented, and those who retained it were said to have learned. The range of human behaviors that was considered teaching was also narrow (lectures and examinations on what was spoken). So, too, was the conception of learning (the echoing of correct answers). In recent years our understanding of teaching and learning has been greatly broadened. Now there are many systems or models of teaching, each with specific strengths and limitations. Also, our concept of what constitutes learning has been expanded to take in a wide range of intellectual, physical, emotional, social, and technological changes.

Our vision of effective teaching therefore has a great deal to do with the kind of knowledge that teachers draw upon as they make day-to-day, minute-by-minute decisions that cumulatively provide the foundation upon which effective teaching is built. In our view, the knowledge shaping these decisions will derive from the individual learners themselves; the culture(s) in which the learning and teaching take place; the body of knowledge about effective teaching in effectively organized schools; and the teacher's knowledge of students, curriculum, instruction, and self. Several "facts" are pertinent here. First, the acts of teaching and learning, particularly as they occur in organizational settings (such as schools and corporations), are a *culturally* defined and influenced phenomena. Schools are human creations like fire departments, symphony orchestras, and professional basketball teams. People put them together in a certain way to do a particular job. Therefore, to be insightful and effective, teachers must not only know themselves but also understand the culture in which they live and work because the culture determines so much of how schools are made. Teachers should be aware of culture's *subtle* influence on their ways of seeing, feeling, and thinking and also be aware of culture's *powerful* influence on the schools in which they will most likely teach.

Despite organizational patterns that place one teacher "in charge" of twenty to thirty learners (in our culture) for a day or an hour, teaching and learning are events and processes that occur between *individuals*. Most significantly, these individuals possess learning and teaching *styles*—patterns of behavior that stem from their individual preferences, needs, and proclivities—that influence the quality of the learning and teaching event. For instance, some students need to see instructions written out, whereas others benefit from hearing them. These cultural and individual facts combine to produce a major element in our vision of effective teaching. For the authors, effective teaching will ultimately and inevitably be the kind of teaching that occurs when a teacher's instructional and curricular decisions are informed by learning style characteristics of students, as well as by an understanding of the cultural, political, and moral dimensions of teaching and learning. Because of the significance and complexity of these factors, individuals seeking to become teachers must commit themselves to becoming persistent, vigorous, proactive learners. Effective teaching is created by energetic "learners" who are constantly bringing new knowledge to bear on their most recent "teaching style."

But we must consider other facts when we begin to describe a vision of effective teaching. Most prominently, a growing body of recommendations and generalizations about good teaching emanates from the "effective teaching" and "effective school" literature, as well as from the multicultural education and critical pedagogy literature, which overlaps with but sometimes challenges the effective teaching literature. The effectiveness literature, moreover, is double-edged. It attempts to define *the reality* of effective teaching by specifying all those things that a teacher will need to be able to do (competencies) before he or she can be certified to be an effective, competent, or hirable teacher. These expected competencies vary from state to state and region to region, but there is an overlap, and our vision of effective teaching incorporates this overlap. We believe that when you see effective teaching in schools anywhere, you will be observing a teacher who possesses one transcendent skill—namely, the ability to synthesize cultural, technical, scientific, curricular, instructional, and self knowledge to create artistic teaching. The activities delineated in this resource text will attempt to put you in touch with educators who are utilizing this skill.

QUESTION 8: **WHAT SHOULD YOU KNOW ABOUT CONTEMPORARY SCHOOLING BEFORE YOU EMBARK ON YOUR OBSERVATION AND INTERVIEWING IN SELECTED SCHOOLS AND SCHOOL DISTRICTS?**

First, realize that your perception of what goes on in school is, in effect, captive of your past experience. Having spent so much time in classrooms as a student makes it difficult for any of us to "see" teaching and learning accurately. If you were to observe how some exotic tribe raises its young or look back at a nineteenth-century British preparatory school, you would bring to the task much fresher, less tainted "eyes." Each of us is a prisoner of our own particular schooling experiences, and this will stand in the way of "seeing" things accurately. In addition, you must recognize that the reality you perceive, and the feelings and thoughts that these perceptions produce, are culturally bound and culturally determined. If you were to walk into a counseling session among a school psychologist, a student, and a parent, and if the school psychologist was performing acupuncture on the student, you would probably be surprised. You might not realize what was taking place because your culture, and your own school experience, had not "prepared" you to "see" acupuncture in American schools.

Second, realize that schools are a social invention that originated relatively recently. As a social invention, they are one way to solve a social problem: "how to introduce the young into productive adult life." And again, as a social invention, they can be replaced or modified or ignored. The essential point, though, is that schools have been "made" by people, and they can be changed by people. As long as people (the taxpayers who pay for schools) are satisfied, schools will remain the same. When people are unhappy with what happens in schools, things will change if the schools exist in a responsive democracy. With this point in mind, as you observe in schools, you should try to discover how the teachers and administrators in selected schools try to keep the public satisfied, and what the consequences are for students.

Third, and related to the preceding issue, what is taught in school is a community's (not the federal government's or the teachers' union's) wager concerning what its children will need to know to live well. Different communities with different social, ethnic, and economic classes make different wagers. Also, some communities guess better than others, and as a result, their children are much better prepared to meet the future. Still, the educational wager is their wager.

Fourth, schools are complex sociopolitical units in which many people, and selected organizations, are important components. Some of them (such as teachers, administrators, and janitors) are seen, and some of them (local school board, banks, publishers, employers, advertisers, state boards of education and key legislators, labor unions such as the National Education Association, and the district superintendent) are not seen. "Seen" or "unseen," each has influence on what happens in classrooms.

All of these components interact to produce the educational reality that you see as well as the educational reality that teachers feel—that is, the morale of a school. When you collect your observational data, you should appreciate that you are skimming the surface of a multilayered, multidimensional organizational network. Indeed, it is as if you were trying to learn about the human body by focusing attention on the eyes, ears, legs, arms, skin, nose, and mouth. These surface features are all quite fascinating and do inform you about the human body, but they do not constitute the entire being. As you look into individual classrooms to learn about the role of teachers and your own possible future in school settings, keep this multidimensional complexity in mind.

Fifth, classrooms and schools are ideas in action. Usually, behind any planned instructional activity is a set of ideas about the nature of human beings, how they learn, what they need to learn, what each child's relationship with others should be, and what are worthy ends of human life. These ideas are not always clearly visible on the surface of the classroom, but rather are embedded in what is being learned and how the teacher organizes what she or he does. Even if the teacher is not fully conscious of these ideas-in-action, they are having an effect. Because of this it is appropriate and helpful to conceive of teaching as a moral endeavor (Goodlad, Soder, and Sirotnick, 1991).

QUESTION 9: **WHY ARE WE ASKING YOU TO OBSERVE IN CLASSROOMS AND, IN PARTICULAR, TO GO TO ALL THE TROUBLE OF INTERVIEWING TEACHERS, PRINCIPALS, AND OTHERS?**

The answer concerns attitudes. Research, as well as the authors' own experience, suggests that a number of potential teachers have unusually romantic, unrealistic notions of what teaching in the modern classroom is all about. For such potential teachers, exposure to professional educators in their workplace becomes a form of career counseling: Potential teachers get an early chance to examine their assumptions about teaching. In addition, there are the important research skills of observing and interviewing, which potential teachers will draw upon during student teaching and throughout their teaching careers. Because of the usefulness and importance of these skills, potential teachers should begin the process of refining their observing and interviewing skills as soon as possible.

At this point you may be ready to ask, "*When* do classroom teachers in general employ these observing and interviewing skills?" The answer is that effective teachers observe their students all of the time in a number of important areas to help make important decisions. They initially observe patterns of verbal and nonverbal behavior and students' leadership in small and large groups. They analyze interactions between child and child and between child and adults. They pick up on unusual reading behaviors (such as eyestrain), listening behaviors (such as straining to hear), and children's emotional state, physical health, and so on. At the same time they also learn about students by interviewing them as well as their parents, former teachers, and members of the community.

The emphasis on interviewing may surprise you somewhat because interviewing is not typically thought of as a teaching task. In fact, however, good teachers need to be good interviewers. Ted Wheeler, a veteran elementary school teacher in San Luis Obispo, California, now retired, made good use of interviewing for many years. He regularly conducted a twenty- to thirty-minute interview with the parents or guardians of each of his students during the first five weeks of school. During this most important first encounter, he asked questions such as these:

1. Tell me a little bit about your child.
2. What responsibilities does your child have at home?
3. What do you do if your child doesn't obey family rules? Does it work?
4. What are some things you'd like your child to learn in our class this year?
5. Do you have any special concerns about the school curriculum?
6. Is your child on any type of medication?
7. Would you be interested in helping the class (or school) as a volunteer?

This type of first conference interview will begin to open trust between parents and teacher; give the teacher up-to-date health and family information (phone number, address, etc.); get more parents involved in public schooling; and set the stage for later three-way conferences among students, parents, and teacher. Teachers can also use in-depth interviews both with students who enter the class later in the year (after the teacher has gone through a good deal of diagnostic activity with students) and other experienced teachers.

Another teacher, Paula McGrath of Dedham, Massachusetts, considers herself a "skilled child watcher." When she meets a new class each fall, she makes a special effort to observe how each child behaves and to observe each child in as many different settings as possible: playground, reading groups, working alone. She records as much of what she sees as soon as possible in anecdotal records for each child—notes to which she returns to think about and to analyze when problems occur.

A third teacher, Chauncey Veatch, who teaches social studies at Coachella Valley High School in Thermal, California, also makes use of interviewing and observational skills. In his teaching, Veatch, who was our National Teacher of the Year in 2002, emphasizes literacy, dreams, and deeply knowing his students and their community. His students are 99 percent Hispanic, and nearly all are from migrant families, with one-third receiving special education services. In his effort to stay in touch with his students' realities and dreams, he implements a yearlong self-disclosure process. Each of his classes begins with a review of what is going on in students' lives, and each presentation is followed by a round of applause. In short, the beginning of each of his classes is part of an ongoing yearlong class interview, and the deep knowing and dream building does not stop at the classroom door. To fill his students with hope and his own cup of knowledge regarding their community, Veatch, on almost every weekend, engages his students in what he calls the "full court press of community involvement." The full court press, among other projects, has brought his students to migrant labor camps, where they disseminated information about health issues, and to elementary schools, where they developed and implemented a literacy buddy program with third-graders. Readers wishing to learn more about Veatch's achievements, as well as the accomplishments of other National Teachers of the Year, can visit the following Web site: www.ccsso.org/projects/National_Teacher_of_the_Year/National_Teachers/127.cfm.

Ted Wheeler, Paula McGrath, and Chauncey Veatch are teachers who put together old and new skills to make themselves outstanding teachers. It is our intention to introduce you to and to provide you practice with this blending of old and new skills. Unlike teachers who have had to develop most of these skills on their own in unstructured situations with little or no feedback on their rates of success, you will be given considerable guidance throughout your student teaching program. With this support in mind, you should be ready to take the first step in developing your skills as a participant observer.

QUESTION 10: **WILL FAITHFULLY COMPLETING ALL THIS WORKBOOK'S ASSIGNMENTS AND EXERCISES GUARANTEE YOUR SUCCESS AS A TEACHER?**

You undoubtedly know the answer to this question already. Sadly, no. However, we guarantee that your faithful engagement in the text and activities will, first, help clarify your career goals, and second, make your further coursework in education more meaningful to you. We say this, however, with one important reservation. You need to add one often "missing ingredient": reflection.

Our everyday lives are filled with experiences. What separates successful people from unsuccessful people is that successful people change their behavior based on their experience. Perhaps they are sarcastic to a friend and discover that the friend shuns them. Therefore, they stop being sarcastic. They party before an important quiz, fail it, and realize they can't do that again. The same truth applies to effective and ineffective teachers. Someone once quipped about a rather ineffective teacher we know. He had announced that he had twenty-four years of teaching experience, and a colleague answered, "Right! You've had one year of teaching experience repeated twenty-four times!" He hadn't grown. He hadn't reflected on his experience, considered alternatives, and changed his behavior.

John Dewey, one of America's major contributors to modern philosophy and author of *Education and Experience* (1938), was a strong advocate of regularly examining our experiences to guide future actions. Dewey believed (p. 38) that "the business of the educator [is] to see in what direction an experience is heading." The current application of Dewey's views is seen in the widespread effort to encourage teachers to be *reflective practitioners*. A reflective practitioner is the opposite of the teacher who repeated his first year of teaching twenty-four times. The reflective practitioner is a teacher with a habit of going back over the events of his or her day to extract meaning from them. Instead of simply letting events wash over them and going on to the next event, reflective practitioners think about teaching *strategically* and modify plans and activities based on past experiences. Again, this is not a one-time happening. It is a well-formed habit that we urge you to begin immediately.

Your various course activities and the ones that are part of this workbook will thrust you into a variety of school-related activities. Some will be familiar, some new and fresh. What is crucial is what you do with that experience. Will you question what you are seeing? Will you reflect on why certain students respond one way and others in an entirely different way? Will you take your impressions and questions to the teacher you are observing or back to the campus for discussion with classmates and your professor? Will you think through how you would have responded to certain situations, such as a student being disruptive? And, ultimately, will you acquire the habits of a reflective practitioner?

A USER'S GUIDE TO *LENSES ON TEACHING*

We have structured this workbook to make your field experiences as educative as possible. From the questions we've posed, you've probably concluded that you will develop several new skills and acquire much useful information and a variety of emerging and existing attitudes and values. To accomplish this, we have structured each of the chapters around a similar format that will facilitate your observations and maximize your attainment of the course objectives.

Although the chapters are sequenced in a manner that reflects both the chronology of your field experiences and the intensity in which you will engage in them, it may be convenient to modify the sequence to match the structure of your unique field experience. In general, the workbook can be resequenced to utilize the unique qualities of your field experience to best advantage.

Each chapter has four parts. The first part of each chapter is a brief essay that will introduce you to the phenomena that should be observed or discovered during that particular visit to the school. The essay will also introduce you to the activities that comprise the "meat" of the chapter. In some cases the activities, which make up the second part of the chapter, are interspersed with the essay, and at other times they stand on their own. The activities are labeled either Core Activity or Suggested Activity. The Core Activities are central to the field experience and should be completed by everyone, whereas the Suggested Activities can be used either in part or in their entirety. The Suggested Activities can augment the Core Activity, provide enrichment activities for individuals or small groups of students, or facilitate the assignment of individual group tasks for large classes.

The third part of each chapter is the Journal Entry, which asks you to reflect upon the observations you've just made and to record your feelings about the phenomena you've observed. This entry should consist of your private thoughts, emerging feelings, new insights, and inner struggles regarding teaching as a career. The journal should be a communication device between you and your instructor, but it may be shared with others, depending upon the course structure. You will find the Journal Entry a useful device for self-exploration.

The fourth part of the chapter is a series of Questions for Discussion. These questions revolve around issues brought up in the essay portion of the chapter and/or around insights that you may have gained from the observations and activities that you completed during that week's field experience. These questions can be responded to orally or in writing, or both, and can also be assigned to specific teams within the class. They provide closure for that set of observations.

Eventually, this part of your journey toward becoming a teacher will end. We hope that this workbook will give you considerable guidance as you complete the journey and ultimately understand your reasons for becoming or not becoming a teacher. The lenses that you acquire as you make this journey will provide you with new ways to look at schools, classrooms, teachers, students, and yourself.

References

Council of Chief State School Officers. (2003, July 11). *Chauncey Veatch, 2002 National Teacher of the Year*. Retrieved from http//www.ccsso.org/projects/National_Teacher_of_the_Year/National_Teachers/127.cfm.

Dewey, John. (1938). *Education and experience.* New York: Macmillan.

Gearing, F., and Hughes, W. (1975). *On observing well: Self-instruction in ethnographic observation for teachers, principals, and supervisors*. Amhurst, NY: Center for Studies of Cultural Transmission, State University of New York at Buffalo.

Goodlad, J. I., Soder, R., and Sirotnick, K. A. (1991). *The moral dimensions of teaching*. San Francisco: Jossey-Bass.

Henry, M. A. (Spring/Summer 1983). The effect of increased exploratory field experiences upon the perceptions and performance of student teachers. *Action in Teacher Education 5*, 66–70.

Jackson, P. (1968). *Life in classrooms*. New York: Holt, Rinehart and Winston.

Popkewitz, T. (1977). *Ideology as a problem of teacher education*. Paper presented at the annual meeting of the American Educational Research Association, New York.

Spradley, J. P., and McCurdy, D. W. (Eds.). (1972). *The cultural experience: Ethnography in complex society*. Chicago: Science Research Associates.

Chapter 2

ORIENTING YOURSELF TO SCHOOLS

Over the next few weeks you will engage in some intensive observation in local elementary schools, junior high or middle schools, and/or high schools. These schools may be located in inner-city areas, urban areas, suburban areas, or rural areas. Some schools may remind you of your own school experiences, whereas others will be utterly foreign to you. Throughout your observations in these schools, you will be sorting out your own feelings about teachers, students, administrators, schools, and ultimately about your decision to become a teacher. In this chapter we provide activities that will orient you to the situation you're observing and enable you to derive more meaningful information from subsequent observations.

You may wonder why you are being asked to spend so much time in schools as part of your teacher preparation program. After all, you've already spent over 16,000 hours in school before you came to college. If quantity of time in classrooms, in and of itself, were sufficient preparation for career decision making, then these initial observations would be superfluous. Yet research has consistently shown that early field experiences are essential both to career decision making and to the development of teaching skills in the areas of instruction and classroom management (Lanier and Little, 1987).

Teachers believe that field experiences were critical to their preparation and frequently bemoan the fact that there aren't more and better experiences prior to student teaching (Lanier and Little, 1987). The issue is how to derive the greatest possible benefit from these field experiences in helping you decide whether to become a teacher, and ultimately in helping you discover the kind of teacher you want to become. By encountering teaching and learning in a variety of contexts and in a wide range of conditions, you will catch glimpses of yourself as a teacher with an emerging teaching style. With the activities in this book, these glimpses will slowly blend into an overall vision that will become increasingly clear to you as you reflect on your own experiences and those of others. Eventually you will feel comfortable in characterizing yourself as a teacher and in taking your first steps toward self-direction and self-development in your career choice.

The first step in this orientation process involves actually visiting and spending considerable time in one or more local schools. Depending on your own school experience, your reaction to this proposition probably ranges somewhere between thrilling and chilling. Your mind will no doubt conjure up images of children happily engaged in activities at workstations, excited buzzing in the hallways, lively discussions in the classroom, and curious learners asking who you are and what you're doing there. You may also visualize faces of kids who are unlike those with whom you went to school, little "rug rats" grabbing you around the leg or throwing up on your shoes, food fights, and the odors that unmistakably tell you that you're "in school."

Myriad questions run through your mind—"What should I wear?" "How should I act?" "Will I really be teaching, or will I be only making copies?" "Whom should I talk to and about what?" "What will I do with my time?" "Do I have to eat lunch there?" "Will the kids accept me, or will they think I'm a jerk?" Don't feel that you're alone in asking these questions. Everyone feels some trepidation when encountering a new experience. What is different is that although you've been in schools before, you haven't looked at them from the perspective of the teacher. It may take you a while to feel comfortable in that role, and the transition may not be easy. The following activities will help you make that transition.

Suggested Activity 1
ARRIVING AT SCHOOL

Upon your arrival at school, someone in authority should greet you and provide background information on the school itself, the expectations that the school's staff has for you, the kinds of experiences that you might expect to have at the school, and some basic ground rules that will make your stay at the school more pleasant. Generally, the person who greets you will be the building principal or assistant principal, although this task is sometimes turned over to others knowledgeable about the school, such as a guidance counselor or head teacher. To gain the most possible information about the school during this orientation, your group may want to ask some of the questions that follow:

ORIENTATION QUESTIONS

1. How many students attend the school, and what is the approximate average class size?
2. How long are class periods (in a high school or junior high school)? How much time do teachers spend on reading, math, science, and social studies (in an elementary school)?
3. Do teachers and students have any free periods (or recess)?
4. What special duties must teachers perform each day or on a regular basis?
5. In your opinion, what makes this school particularly pleasant to work in?
6. Are there special rules or policies that help make the school run smoothly?
7. Are there particular activities or achievements for which the school is well known in the area?
8. Has the school building or the school environment undergone any noteworthy changes or improvements recently?
9. How diverse is the student population? Does that present any special challenges to the staff?
10. Are there any areas or activities that you would especially like us to observe while we're in your school?

After your introduction to the school, you may find that you've formed strong initial impressions of the school. Based on the sights, sounds, and smells that you've encountered, you're probably sensing or feeling a "comfort level" within which you'll be able to operate in this building. You are probably experiencing sensations that are telling you areas that you want to visit, areas that you want to avoid, people whom you want to find out more about, students whom you want to observe more extensively, and so forth. These initial impressions will have a significant impact on your first few observations and, to some extent, will "frame" that experience by providing a context within which to interpret your experiences.

For that reason, it is important for you to elicit your initial impressions of the school and to write them down for closer examination. The process of writing them down will help you to understand the feelings that you're having about schools and about teaching. They will also provide a useful point of reference to return to after you've completed *all* of your observations. You may be surprised to discover how your feelings have varied from the beginning of your observations to the end.

Suggested Activity 2

INITIAL IMPRESSIONS OF SCHOOL BUILDING

For this activity you should use the following worksheet to record your initial impressions of the school. Many of your statements will resemble a "free association" as you link a sensation with an impression. That's a logical way to talk to yourself as you're walking around the building or listening to an orientation session. It is important that you move from those impressions based on sensations to a set of conclusions based on your impressions. As soon as possible after you've completed Part 1 of this activity, try to complete Part 2.

PART 1: MY INITIAL IMPRESSIONS OF THE SCHOOL

1. _____

   _____

2. _____

   _____

3. _____

   _____

4. _____

   _____

5. _____

   _____

6. _____

   _____

7. _____

   _____

8. _____

   _____

9. _____

   _____

10. _____

    _____

**PART 2: WHAT DO MY IMPRESSIONS LEAD ME TO CONCLUDE
ABOUT THE SCHOOL?**

1. Conclusions about the building: _____

   _____

   _____

   _____

2. Conclusions about the administration: _____

   _____

   _____

   _____

3. Conclusions about the teachers: _____

   _____

   _____

   _____

4. Conclusions about the students: _____

   _____

   _____

   _____

5. Conclusions about the community: _____

   _____

   _____

   _____

   Now that you have formed some conclusions about the nature of the school
building and how it operates, try to respond to specific questions about the school as
though you were being interviewed by someone who had never visited this school
before. Be as vivid and descriptive as possible in your responses.

Suggested Activity 3*
DESCRIBING THE SCHOOL

---

1. Describe the physical characteristics of this school. Is the building old or new? What are the exterior and the grounds like? Does the building appear inviting? How is it decorated inside? Are certain areas carpeted? What impression do you get from these physical facilities?

    _____

    _____

    _____

    _____

2. From what you observed, can you tell who is in charge? What incidents have you observed that suggest that some individuals have control over others?

    _____

    _____

    _____

    _____

3. How do people dress in this school? Are there differences among the various groups of people?

    _____

    _____

    _____

    _____

4. Is there a central or official place where authority resides? What are some things you observed that led to your conclusion?

    _____

    _____

    _____

    _____

---

*(Ryan, Burkholder, and Phillips, 1983).

5. Are some places more physically comfortable than others? Who gets to use them?

_____

_____

_____

_____

6. How are the students working? What are they doing? Are they working singly or in groups? Are they quiet? Or are they talking freely?

_____

_____

_____

_____

7. Is there a special area for public displays? If so, what is in them, and what do they say about this school? Go into the teachers' lounge(s) and places where teachers eat and observe the physical facilities, the information on the bulletin boards, the behavior of individuals, and if and how that behavior differs from "public" behavior. What are some of the topics that people talk about?

_____

_____

_____

_____

8. Finally, report anything that happened to you in the process of making the observations. This includes encounters with people or questions about what you were doing. Also, comment on things that you expected to happen that did not. Conclude by giving your general impressions of the school that you visited.

_____

_____

_____

_____

Are the classrooms you are observing organized to enhance student learning?

"And then, of course, there's the possibility of being just the slightest bit too organized."

Glen Dines KAPPAN
Holt, Rinehart and Winston

Although school buildings have a considerable amount of commonality, classrooms are quite diverse in the way that they are arranged, decorated, and used. Classrooms appear to have a personality, and that personality is a curious blend of the teacher's style and the students' needs and values. Classrooms offer interesting contrasts in both form and function. Some classrooms appear to be living spaces, whereas others appear to be places where people work. Some are vividly decorated and vibrant in tone, whereas others are stark and uninviting. Although elementary classrooms generally seem more inviting than secondary classrooms, some secondary classrooms excite both the senses and the imagination. However, because secondary teachers often move from room to room in their day's teaching, the cumulative effect is that secondary classrooms lack the fine touches that will often accumulate in stimulating ways in elementary classrooms.

Because the bulk of your observation time will be spent in the classroom, there should be ample opportunity to sketch a detailed map that depicts where the teacher and students are located as well as unique features of the room's organization. Besides showing the physical layout of the classroom, identify the more subtle features as

well. For example, is the room lighted naturally or artificially? Are desks designed for mobility? Does the physical arrangement of the desks facilitate the use of a variety of teaching strategies? Are bulletin boards or displays coordinated with the unit or course content? Is media hardware (e.g., televisions, computers, overhead projectors, screens) located in such a way as to enhance instruction and learning (Emmer et al., 1983)?

Next is an "aerial" view of an empty classroom. Use this space to illustrate the classroom you're observing. Include as much detail as possible.

Core Activity
MAPPING THE CLASSROOM

Student Name: _____ Date: _____

Based on your map, respond to the following questions:

1. In what ways is the organization of the classroom conducive to student learning? In what ways does it inhibit learning?

_____

_____

_____

_____

2. Given this classroom organization, what would you expect to be important elements of the teacher's philosophy or style of teaching?

_____

_____

_____

_____

3. Do the students and the teacher appear comfortable with the classroom organization? On what do you base this conclusion?

_____

_____

_____

_____

4. If you were the teacher, how would you modify this classroom to fit your style of teaching?

_____

_____

_____

_____

During this first visit to the school, you've encountered many individuals who made an impression on you. These individuals may have included an administrator who introduced you to the school building and to your cooperating teacher, the classroom teacher whom you observed, or a student (or students) to whom you were drawn throughout the observation. Or these individuals could have been people on the school staff such as the office secretary, a maintenance worker, or a cafeteria helper. Over the next few weeks these individuals may have a considerable impact on your decision to become a teacher, and it will be useful to think about how these people might affect your perceptions of schools, teaching, and learning.

Based on this initial contact, try to identify the person who made the *most vivid* impression on you and analyze why she or he affected you this way. The impression may have been either positive or negative, but the critical element is to discern how this individual might alter or enhance your perceptions of a career in teaching. Use the form that follows to describe, analyze, and evaluate the impression that this individual made on you.

Suggested Activity 4

THE MOST MEMORABLE PERSON

---

1. Description of the person who made the most vivid impression on me (include in this description the role that this person had in the school, how you interacted with him or her, and a brief discussion of what he or she did to make such a vivid impression on you):

    _____

    _____

    _____

    _____

2. Analysis of why this person might affect your perceptions of the school (include in this analysis a description of how this person affected you, in what way she or he altered your perceptions, and why she or he might influence your decisions about teaching):

    _____

    _____

    _____

    _____

3. Evaluation of the person who impressed you most vividly (include in this evaluation your feelings about why this person might influence you, what you've discovered about yourself through interacting with this person, and whether you should allow your perceptions to be influenced by him or her):

    _____

    _____

    _____

    _____

Your first observation in the school has left you with a variety of feelings, some vivid impressions, and a tremendous number of questions. Use these feelings, impressions, and questions to generate a list of things that you would like to do or see in your remaining observations. The Journal Entry that follows is a logical place to include this list as well as to record a few of your reactions to your first visit to the school. Because this is your first Journal Entry, you should complete it as soon as possible after your visit to the school.

Student Name: _____ Date: _____

Journal Entry

Because this is your first Journal Entry based on your first impressions of the school and of the teacher(s) whom you are observing, use those impressions as the focal point of this entry. Concentrate on the school structure, its functional nature, and its aesthetic qualities. How do you feel about the school and the conditions under which teaching and learning occur? What are your initial impressions of the teacher's workload? How would you summarize your feelings about teaching right now?

_____

_____

_____

_____

_____

_____

_____

_____

_____

_____

_____

_____

_____

_____

_____

_____

_____

Questions for Discussion

1. Based on your initial observations, what are your impressions of the school and its role in the education of the community? What are your impressions of the teacher and his or her role(s) in the school? Did those impressions change during your observation? Why?

2. Critically analyze your impressions of the school. What aspects of the school made the biggest impression on you? Were most of your impressions positive or negative? How might these impressions affect later observations?

3. Critically analyze the classroom that you observed in terms of its physical arrangement. In what ways is the physical arrangement conducive to teaching and learning? In what ways is it detrimental? If this were your classroom, how would you change it?

4. Describe your feelings as you walked around the school. What impressed you regarding its physical structure, organization, resources, aesthetics, and so forth? What did you dislike about it? Did you see the school as inviting or discouraging learning? In what ways might your impressions change during subsequent observations?

References

Emmer, E. T., Evertson, C. M., Sanford, J. P., Clements, B. S., and Worsham, M. E. (1983). *Organizing and managing the junior high school classroom* (pp. 6-15). University of Texas at Austin: The Research and Development Center for Teacher Education.

Lanier, J., and Little, J. (1987). Research on teacher education. In Merlin C. Wittrock (Ed.), *Handbook of research on teaching* (3rd ed.) (pp. 550-552). New York: Macmillan.

Ryan, K., Burkholder, S., and Phillips, D. H. (1983). *The workbook: Exploring careers in teaching* (pp. 49-50). Columbus, OH: Merrill.

Chapter 3

CONTEMPORARY PRACTICES AND ISSUES IN TEACHING AND LEARNING

During your first observations you were able to record some impressions of the school building, its classrooms, a teacher's workday, and to some extent the role of the administrator. Chances are that with little effort you synthesized these impressions and decided whether your assigned school was using "best practices" or not. You based this conclusion largely on how *you* would like a school to operate and on how closely this school's operation matched your ideal. Perhaps you felt the elementary or high school from which you graduated operated effectively, and that because this school's operation closely mirrored your own school, it must be using "best practices." These conclusions are useful because they help us frame our experiences and provide guidance as to the kind of school settings in which we'd feel comfortable working.

In the long term, however, conclusions are helpful only if the evidence they're based on is solid. Initial impressions, though powerful, can be misleading. In this chapter you will be given structured activities that will help you collect evidence on innovative practices that may be occurring in the school(s) that you are observing. This evidence may support or refute your initial impressions; but more important, it will strengthen your propensity to rigorously evaluate the evidence on which you base your conclusions.

BEST PRACTICES IN TODAY'S CLASSROOMS

In Chapter 4 you will observe classroom teachers, systematically collect data on their teaching strategies and techniques, and draw conclusions about which strategies and techniques you would like to develop and use in your own classroom. In some cases these strategies and techniques may be best practices, meaning that they are based on and derived from solid research on effective teaching. In other cases, however, you may be impressed with a technique that may seem to work at the moment the teacher uses it in the classroom. What you need to reflect on is whether the latter technique can be replicated under different conditions and with a different teacher or if that technique was effective only for that particular classroom event or a particular type of teaching personality. Being able to sort out and discriminate the research-based best practice from the narrow, situation-specific successful technique will help you build your own personal theory of teaching and learning. What seems to work in a particular case may not always be a best practice in every context.

Teachers in today's schools have been influenced in their teacher preparation and professional development programs by two competing and at times complementary philosophies: behaviorism and constructivism. From the early 1960s to the mid-1980s, behaviorism dominated both teacher preparation programs and the research on effective teaching. From the mid-1980s to the present, constructivism has emerged as an increasingly influential philosophy both in teacher preparation programs and in professional development activities, particularly in mathematics and science education, early childhood education, and reading/language arts education. Rooted in the progressive philosophy of John Dewey and the research of developmental psychologists such as Jean Piaget, Jerome Bruner, and Lev Vygotsky, constructivism may appear at first to be antithetical to behaviorism. Although the philosophies represent different perspectives on how children learn to think and behave, effective teachers can draw from both in constructing a learning environment that invites learners to succeed. To illustrate, examine Table 3.1 and analyze the similarities and differences among a

TABLE 3.1
Philosophical Perspectives on Learning Environments

	Behaviorism (DeMar, 1997)	**Constructivist (Henriques, 2002)**	**Blended**
Learning environment	Teacher controlled; students respond to stimuli presented by the teacher; teacher designs the environment to maximize desired responses from the student.	Teacher structures environment with input from students; students control own behavior; students construct meaning from experiences embedded in the learning environment.	Teacher structures an environment that maximizes opportunity for desired behaviors to be performed and meaning to be constructed from those experiences.
Student	Responds to environment; establishes pattern of behavior that demonstrates ability to form and develop concepts and skills as determined by an external "authority" (that is, the content the teacher provides); responds positively to rewards given by the teacher, the environment, or both.	Viewed as a "thinker" with emerging theories about the world; provides interpretive constructions of concepts and skills that the teacher builds on in subsequent lessons; students pose questions rather than responding to them; establishes internal reward system based on satisfaction derived from understanding and appreciating experiences.	Sees the importance of and need for correct responses and the need to ask good questions; uses information acquired from the content as a foundation to build on in constructing meaning from experience; requires both external symbols of success and internal reward systems.

TABLE 3.1
(*continued*)

	Behaviorism (DeMar, 1997)	Constructivist (Henriques, 2002)	Blended
Teacher	Disseminates information and provides experiences for students; selects and structures the curriculum and learning experiences; uses learning principles of reinforcement, repetition, and contiguity in a planned, systematic approach to instruction; expects student responses to be similar, although not always the same.	Guides and facilitates learning; creates an environment with few if any correct answers but expects students to challenge, deconstruct, and reconstruct the curriculum; uses interpretation and construction of meaning from experience as primary learning principle; designs basic lesson plan, but student voice plays an important role in determining the course of the lesson; expects divergent, not identical, responses from learners.	Directs lessons to establish a conceptual, informational base, but transitions to a student-directed format when appropriate; works from established curriculum but connects students' experiences to the curriculum and vice versa; enables predictable and creative responses to performances; uses both behaviorist and constructivist theories of teaching and learning as appropriate to the context.
Assessment	Measurable and/or observable, usually involving a performance assessed against a standard benchmark or a paper-and-pencil response; teacher made or standardized and usually quantifiable; responses should be the same as or similar to the model provided; usually follows instruction.	Usually qualitative and may involve teacher observations of students at work, portfolios, or exhibitions; performance may be assessed by a rubric, but unique responses or interpretations must be incorporated; use of authentic assessments is encouraged; is usually embedded in instruction rather than following instruction; teacher determines *why* a certain response was made rather than just assessing the response.	Contextual and may involve the ability to demonstrate knowledge of important information as well as use and transfer concepts and skills to new contexts; uses both authentic and paper-and-pencil assessments; embedded in the context but may occur during or after instruction; teacher expects correct responses and also wants to know *why* students responded as they did.

TABLE 3.2

Comparison of Traditional and Constructivist Classrooms

Traditional Classroom	Constructivist Classroom
Curriculum begins with the parts of the whole; emphasizes basic skills.	Curriculum emphasizes big concepts, beginning with the whole and expanding to include the parts.
Strict adherence to fixed curriculum is highly valued.	Pursuit of student questions and interests is valued.
Materials are primarily textbooks and workbooks.	Materials include primary sources of material and hands-on activities.
Learning is based on repetition.	Learning is interactive, building on what the student already knows.
Teachers disseminate information to students; students are recipients of knowledge.	Teachers have a dialogue with students, helping students construct their own knowledge.
Teacher's role is directive, rooted in authority.	Teacher's role is interactive, rooted in negotiation.
Assessment is through testing, correct answers.	Assessment includes student works, observations, and points of view, as well as tests. Process is as important as product.
Knowledge is seen as inert.	Knowledge is seen as dynamic, ever changing with our experiences.
Students work primarily alone.	Students work primarily in groups.

purely behaviorist approach to teaching and learning, a constructivist approach to teaching and learning, and a blended approach to teaching and learning.

Although each of the perspectives in Table 3.1 contains elements of best practices, the effective teacher will have more opportunity to use best practices in the blended classroom. However, you may not be totally comfortable with blending these two philosophies as you think about your own teaching and how you would construct a learning environment. You may be most familiar with a traditional classroom because that's the learning environment you experienced most frequently in your own K–12 and even college education. You may have also experienced some constructivist classrooms and either didn't realize it or didn't feel particularly comfortable in that environment. Table 3.2 compares a traditional and a constructivist classroom. Determine which one you have experienced more frequently, which one you felt more comfortable in, and which one you would more likely draw on as you create your own classroom environment.

Now that you have had the opportunity to consider and compare the behaviorist, constructivist, and blended teaching perspectives and the traditional and constructivist classroom environments, complete the Core Activity for this chapter.

Core Activity

IDEAL LEARNING ENVIRONMENT

As individuals or in small groups, describe the kind of learning environment that you feel best represents your vision of the ideal learning environment. Keep in mind that your vision doesn't necessarily have to look like the present *school building* that we currently use as a learning environment.

_____

_____

_____

_____

_____

_____

_____

MY MODEL FOR THE IDEAL LEARNING ENVIRONMENT

Role of the teacher (describe what the "teacher" does in your model and *who* the teacher is):

_____

_____

_____

_____

Role of the learner (describe what the "learner" does in your model and *who* the learner is):

_____

_____

_____

_____

Curriculum to be learned (describe what will be learned in your model and *who* decides the curriculum):

_____

_____

_____

_____

Methods of teaching/learning (describe how the curriculum will be taught and learned):

_____

_____

_____

_____

Organization of the learning environment (describe how the learning environment will be managed and by whom):

_____

_____

_____

_____

CONTEMPORARY ISSUES IN TODAY'S CLASSROOMS

Schools today are affected by a variety of social forces over which educators have little control or influence (Eisner, 1979). These forces are usually grounded in the economy, politics, the media, and legal debates. Although this is not an exhaustive list, such forces include school funding, national standardized tests, charter schools, violence in schools (including bullying), and constitutional debates such as the one pertaining to separation of church and state. You may have experienced the effects of some of these forces yourself as a student, but it is unlikely that you have considered them from the perspective of the teacher or school administrator. The following sections briefly describe some contemporary issues and forces in schools. After discussing these issues and forces, you can use the Suggested Activities to help you analyze the impact they might have on your own teaching and the learning environments you want to create.

School Funding

One of the most perplexing problems facing taxpayers and politicians is how to fund schools to ensure that students in K–12 public schools are supported equitably and adequately. As will be seen in our discussion of the No Child Left Behind Act of 2001 in Chapter 6, the federal government claims that it is providing more funding than ever to support the mandates of NCLB. However, state legislators and school administrators are virtually unanimous in asserting that NCLB is underfunded like other federal mandates such as Head Start and the Individuals with Disabilities Act (IDEA). In fact, one state, Connecticut, is suing the federal government, claiming that its schools cannot meet NCLB mandates given the level of funding provided, and it is seeking to prevent the federal government from enforcing those mandates (Gillespie, 2005).

In other states such as Ohio, individuals, with the support of groups concerned about the way schools are funded in the state, have taken their cases to the state supreme courts seeking to force state legislatures to create an equitable and adequate funding system for schools. The *DeRolph* case, first brought to the state supreme court in 1997, sought to force the legislature to create a funding system that met the "thorough and efficient" standard established in Section 2 of Article VI of the Ohio Constitution (Ohio School Funding, 2003). Over the next three years the state legislature tried to design a funding formula to meet this standard, but by 2000 the Ohio Supreme Court ruled in a 4–3 decision that the state had failed to do this and declared that the state's system for funding schools was unconstitutional. This decision, known as *DeRolph II,* upheld the 1997 ruling in *DeRolph I* and further directed the state legislature to solve the problem and create a funding system that met the standards set forth in the state's constitution by June 15, 2001 (Ohio School Funding, 2003). Unfortunately, the elections of 2002 changed the membership of the state supreme court and the legislature, and to this date the funding formula has not been changed. It is noteworthy that the efforts of Ohio citizens and organizations in 1997 to create more equity in the state funding of public schools was not an isolated phenomenon. For example, in 1989 lawyers for plaintiffs in Kentucky, Texas, Montana, New Jersey, and Wisconsin were successful in persuading their respective state supreme courts to declare their school finance systems unconstitutional (Verstegen, 1994). And in Wyoming in 1995, and Alabama and Vermont in 1997, the school finance systems in these states were also declared unconstitutional (White, 1997). There are many more examples, as your research will demonstrate.

Because states rely on a variety of taxes to fund schools—from real estate taxes to property taxes to income taxes to sales taxes or some combination of all of these— there is an inconsistency across the United States in how schools are funded and whether this funding is adequate to meet the needs of *all* students in *all* school districts. In Suggested Activity 1 you will identify how schools are funded in your state and whether that system is considered both adequate and equitable across all school districts in the state.

Charter Schools

Although charter schools have been around for a number of years, they were given a considerable boost with the passage of the No Child Left Behind Act of 2001. In giving parents the choice to move their children from low-performing schools, NCLB also included charter schools as one option parents could choose. Charter schools can provide a wide variety of options to students because they can be organized around specific themes, skill areas, location, or the like. Thus, for example, there are charter schools that integrate content fields through the arts, through vocational skills centers, and through museum-based programs.

Charter schools tend to be run by parents, community groups, and educators and supported by private funding as well as state subsidy (Schnaiberg, 1997). The latter source of funding has troubled superintendents and school boards in public schools, especially in urban areas. When parents send their children to a charter school, the state subsidy follows those children to the charter school and away from the public school district. In some urban districts this has resulted in the loss of millions of dollars and, with lower enrollment, has also meant that some schools have closed. Further, the loss in subsidy has forced districts to go back to taxpayers to recapture the lost revenues by increasing taxes. This scenario has left public school officials critical of charter schools, and they largely blame the NCLB Act for imposing this situation on public schools. This, coupled with the lack of evidence that charter school students actually perform better than their counterparts in the public schools on standardized state proficiency tests, leaves public school officials wondering if charter schools are really the answer to improving educational performance (Sandham, 2001).

There is no question that charter schools specifically and school choice in general are putting pressure on public schools to demonstrate that they can perform well enough to maintain parents' and taxpayers' confidence in their ability to educate students successfully. Whether this is perceived as healthy competition or government-imposed punishment for forces schools can't control depends on whether you are an advocate for or a critic of charter schools and school choice. As you analyze this force affecting education today, be sure to gather evidence and weigh arguments from both sides of this issue. Try to determine if charter schools are a challenge or a threat to public education and to the future of public schools.

Violence in Schools

Since the 1970s the media, the public, and many educators have become more aware of and alarmed about school violence. In the middle to late 1990s these fears were fueled by the tragic incidents in Jonesboro, Arkansas, and Littleton, Colorado, in which students brought guns to school and killed classmates and teachers. Despite these perceptions and tragic events, schools are generally considered safer than any other environment in which children live and play (Hyman and Perone, 1998). An individual is five times more likely to be the victim of assault in his or her neighborhood than in school, for example (Hyman and Perone, 1998). However, most educators would agree that any incident of violence in school is too much. What is less obvious is how to reduce or prevent these cases of violence and the degree to which educators themselves contribute to creating an atmosphere in which violence can occur in schools.

As Hyman and Perone note, school administrators have tended to turn to law enforcement methods rather than educational models to reduce or prevent violence in schools (Hyman and Perone, 1998). Such methods as metal detectors, student and teacher identification badges, greater police presence in schools, locker searches, and even school uniforms have been generally shown to be ineffective in preventing or reducing violence in schools (Hyman and Perone, 1998).

If law enforcement methods are generally ineffective, then what other options are available to school administrators? Some researchers have suggested that educational models may be the answer (Berson and Berson, 1999). Others say the size of the school may be a factor in school violence and suggest that either smaller schools or building smaller "communities" within schools may be the answer (Raywid and Oshiyama, 2000). Whether in a smaller school setting or in communities within schools, several educational models seem to provide a promising alternative to traditional law enforcement methods. These include programs that promote problem solving, social skills training, anger management, conflict resolution, strong family bonds, greater communication, and youth mentoring, among others (Berson and Berson, 1999).

One of the more promising of these educational programs is the antibullying program supported and promoted by Peter Yarrow (of the singing group Peter, Paul, and Mary) and initially marketed under the title "Don't Laugh at Me!" Bullying in schools has always been a problem, but the link between bullying behavior and the violence at Columbine High School and Jonesboro Middle School has brought renewed attention to this problem. It has been estimated by the National Education Association that 160,000 students miss school each day because of incidents related to bullying (Chiarelott, 2006). Many of these incidents could be prevented by educators (Hyman and Perone, 1998). The issue of student victimization by school staff is often overlooked when people consider the causes of violent behavior among students who act aggressively and violently toward school staff members as well as their peers (Hyman and Perone, 1998). The use of corporal punishment by teachers and administrators is generally seen as one of the major contributors to aggressive responses by students; also included in this list are behaviors such as inappropriate teasing, taunting, verbally aggressive threats, and teachers ignoring students' aggressive behavior toward other students including physical threats, sexual harassment, homophobic remarks, and the like.

As you consider the issue of violence in schools in completing Suggested Activity 1, examine both the causes and potential solutions. What can educators do not only to prevent violence but also to educate students on how to handle problems so that violence is not the solution they choose? Analyze the extent to which bullying exists in schools and how educators might be contributing to an atmosphere of bullying and aggressive behavior in schools. Finally, evaluate the myths and misconceptions about school violence and how it can best be reduced or prevented.

Constitutional Issues: The Separation of Church and State

Teachers today face increasing pressure from groups and organizations that either want an increased emphasis on morality and religion in schools or want those topics totally removed from the classroom and the curriculum. As in many issues of this type, no extreme position is viable. Morality and references to religion can be neither the primary focus of the curriculum nor completely eliminated.

Supported by a variety of organizations and foundations such as the Eagle Forum and the Rutherford Institute, a wide range of religious groups, usually fundamentalist Christian in orientation, have challenged the traditional separation of church and state as practiced by most public schools. In some states this has resulted in the inclusion of "intelligent design" in the science curriculum to offset the perceived exclusion of a supreme being in the teaching of evolution. In California, for example, a group representing California's religious schools has filed a lawsuit against the University of California system for allegedly discriminating against high schools that teach creationism and other conservative Christian perspectives. The suit centers on the UC system's refusal to certify high school science courses that use textbooks that challenge Darwin's theory of evolution (Suit alleges, August 28, 2005).

Because of opposition from representatives of influential organizations such as the American Civil Liberties Union (ACLU), the American Association for the Advancement of Science (AAAS), and the National Education Association (NEA), religious, legal, and educational groups frequently find themselves at odds over how topics of religion and morality should be handled in the schools. At issue is the "establishment" clause of the U.S. Constitution, which forbids the federal government from imposing a particular religion or religious belief on the citizens of the United States.

Schools and the school curriculum are increasingly becoming the battleground between individuals and groups who want to see a greater emphasis on religion (especially Christianity) and morality in schools and the individuals and groups who oppose them. As you consider this issue in Suggested Activity 1, investigate guidelines that have been approved and supported by legal, educational, and religious groups and identify what these guidelines include as constitutionally appropriate religious activities in the school. Debate whether these guidelines provide a clear sense of direction for teachers and administrators in public schools. Finally, determine what you believe would be an appropriate way to deal with issues of religion and morality in public schools—grades P–6 and grades 7–12.

Standardized Tests

As we note in the discussion of the No Child Left Behind Act of 2001 in Chapter 6 (and earlier in this chapter in the discussion of charter schools), school leaders are under increasing pressure to demonstrate measurable improvement in students' performance on standardized tests each year. Although this type of accountability is not new, these so-called high-stakes tests are stirring up considerable controversy.

Supporters of the testing movement argue that without some kind of norm-referenced testing, it is impossible to compare students' and schools' ability to meet state and federal standards. Further, they argue, these tests need to have some "teeth" or there would be no reason for students, teachers, school administrators, and school boards to take them seriously. Without some kind of consequence for poor performance (e.g., replacing staff, changing the curriculum, reducing funding, privatizing the management of the school, allowing parents to move their children to higher-performing schools) the status quo would prevail, and some schools might even get worse with no consequences. Furthermore, because the tests are standardized and based on the approved curriculum for each content area, proponents argue that such tests provide the fairest and most productive strategy for assessing school performance.

Opponents to the use of standardized tests to gauge school effectiveness decry the overemphasis on testing and the time and financial resources it takes away from instruction and student learning. A frequently cited aphorism used by standardized testing opponents, "You don't fatten up cattle by constantly weighing them," suggests that the time teachers take in preparing students for the tests and administering them doesn't make students smarter. That time would be better spent teaching the students new concepts and skills.

Another point of concern cited by opponents of standardized testing is the extent to which the tests drive the curriculum rather than the reverse. They suggest that teachers now rarely design and develop curriculum. They must teach to the areas covered in the standardized proficiency tests, typically in a manner that has little to do with self-directed learning and creative thinking. While supporters argue that the tests are based on what's in the state-approved curriculum, opponents argue the opposite—the state-approved curriculum is derived from the concepts and skills measured on the test.

As you analyze the effect standardized tests have on the school curriculum, weigh the balance between teacher accountability and teacher autonomy. To what extent should teachers be allowed to influence or determine *what* is taught in their classrooms? To what extent should their autonomy be limited to *how* content is taught rather than determining the actual content? Should teachers be held accountable for their students' performance? To what extent should that accountability be related to the school's success overall and the teachers' retention of their positions?

Suggested Activity 1

CONTEMPORARY ISSUES

This activity will allow you to develop expertise in one of the issues affecting schools and teachers discussed in this chapter while also gaining information on the other areas. To complete this activity, follow these procedures:

PROCEDURES

1. Divide the class into five groups of five students each. If the class is smaller than twenty-five, determine which issues are the most compelling and set up two, three, or four groups of five students. If there are more than twenty-five students in the class, set up as many groups of five students as needed so that each student is in a group.

2. Have each group discuss the issues briefly, and have group members assign at least one student to each issue.

3. Reconstitute the groups so that there are five students assigned to each issue (school violence, standardized testing, separation of church and state/constitutional issues, school funding, and charter schools).

4. Provide adequate time for each "expert" group to collect data and review research on each issue. This may be assigned as an out-of-class responsibility or done during class time.

5. After each group has completed research and data collection, have the expert groups meet and combine their findings. Each member of the expert group should have a compilation of research and information that constitutes the collected wisdom of the expert group.

6. Have the members of the expert groups return to their original groups. Allow time for each group member to share his or her area of expertise with the other group members and provide handouts summarizing their groups' findings if possible. The group should be allowed time to discuss each issue in depth.

7. Following the small group assignment, each group member should write a brief (250–500 word) summary discussing each issue and describing which issue she or he would find most troubling to handle as a teacher.

PROFESSIONAL DEVELOPMENT SCHOOLS

Since the late 1980s teacher education programs and pre-K–12 schools have been working together to help prepare preservice teachers and to provide ongoing professional development to practicing teachers. Dubbed *professional development schools* (PDSs), these partnerships first appeared as a recommendation of the Holmes Group, which was a collection of research-oriented institutions of higher education that also had some commitment to teacher education. The concept was further endorsed by John Goodlad in a set of "postulates" that he proposed to reconceptualize the process of teacher education. More recently, the Holmes Group has expanded its base to include institutions with a strong tradition of preparing teachers and working closely with local education associations (LEAs) that have also been interested in restructuring the manner in which they develop their existing teaching staff. This expanded group is called the Holmes Partnership, and it is encouraging the creation of ongoing collaborative relationships between teacher preparation institutions and LEAs.

The PDS partnerships have been described as "exemplars of practice, builders of knowledge, and vehicles for sharing professional learning among educators with an emphasis on putting research into practice and practice into research" (Metcalf-Turner and Fischetti, 1996). In a sense, this model is attempting to "simultaneously renew" pre-K–12 schools and programs of teacher education. Supporters of PDS point out that it does little good to reform schools if we continue to turn out traditional teachers or to develop innovative teachers and then place them into ineffective schools.

Supporters of PDS also suggest that the assumption that one becomes a teacher after completing a teacher preparation program is erroneous. A teacher is always in the process of *becoming,* and the journey lasts for an entire career. The concept of ongoing professional development (1) beginning with the preservice teacher preparation program in conjunction with a strong liberal arts background, (2) continuing through entry-year or fifth-year "induction" into the profession, and (3) culminating with a career-long commitment to ongoing professional growth is an essential element of PDS.

Your teacher preparation program may be part of a PDS partnership, or it may be in the process of developing some formal or informal relationships. Here are some common elements of these types of relationships:

- A teamlike organizational structure with four to five classroom teachers, two to three university professors, five to ten graduate interns, several teacher candidates, and others with appropriate areas of expertise serving as resource people (Metcalf-Turner and Fischetti, 1996).
- A long-term, ongoing field placement at a particular site that exemplifies "best practices" and involves teacher candidates as part of a teaching team in the school.
- On-site teaching by university faculty and/or adjunct faculty from the LEA and a concomitant exchange in which classroom teachers provide on-campus learning experiences.
- Assessment of teacher candidates' learning through a variety of strategies appropriate to that site and the needs of the candidates.

- An ongoing commitment of the college to the PDS so that the partnership ultimately benefits the community and enhances the achievement of the students in the pre-K–12 setting.

Although this list is hardly exhaustive, it represents some of the major premises on which PDS partnerships are built. As a result, both the college faculty and the classroom teachers should experience considerable growth in their own teaching skills, increased understanding of the art and science of teaching, and an improved appreciation for each other's areas of expertise.

As you begin your journey to becoming a teacher, it is essential that you understand that you will never stop learning. In terms of your preservice teacher preparation and the school(s) in which you find yourself teaching, you should choose situations that encourage high-quality professional development. The National Foundation for the Improvement of Education (1996) has summarized the characteristics of a high-quality professional development program:

- Has the goal of improving student learning at the heart of every school endeavor.
- Helps teachers and other school staff meet the future needs of students who learn in different ways and who come from diverse cultural, linguistic, and socioeconomic backgrounds.
- Provides adequate time for inquiry, reflection, and mentoring and is an important part of the normal working day of all public school educators.
- Is rigorous, sustained, and adequate to the long-term change of practice.
- Is directed toward teachers' intellectual development and leadership.
- Fosters a deepening of subject matter knowledge, a greater understanding of learning, and a greater appreciation of students' needs.
- Is designed and directed by teachers, incorporates the best principles of adult learning, and involves shared decisions designed to improve the school.
- Balances individual priorities with school and district needs and advances the profession as a whole.
- Makes the best use of new technologies.
- Is site-based and supportive of a clearly articulated vision for students.

An important aspect of your exploration of the teaching profession should be the examination of your own education and how well you are prepared to continue learning throughout your career. As part of your discussion of professional development with your campus-based instructor, your classmates, your cooperating teacher(s), and others enrolled in the program, you may want to seek answers to the questions in Suggested Activity 2.

Suggested Activity 2

EXPLORING YOUR OWN PROFESSIONAL DEVELOPMENT

1. What opportunities do you have in your teacher preparation program to observe and interview practicing teachers?
2. How central is the process of "reflective teaching" to the clinical and field experiences in which you are required to participate?
3. When in your program do you encounter a practicing teacher who serves as your mentor?
4. How *connected* are your field experiences with each other, and how *integrated* are they with your campus-based activities?
5. How and when in your teacher education program is your growth as a teacher assessed, and how do you learn to assess the outcomes established for your students?
6. What options for further professional development do you have after completing your teacher preparation program and receiving your teaching license/certificate?
7. How do your mentor teacher and cooperating teachers stay up-to-date professionally? What have been their most satisfying and useful professional development experiences since they became teachers?

Student Name: _____ Date: _____

Journal Entry

_____

_____

_____

_____

_____

_____

_____

_____

_____

_____

_____

Questions for Discussion

1. How will you determine if a teacher is using "best practices" in the classroom? What might you ask the teacher to determine if she or he has a well-articulated philosophy of teaching?

2. What criteria did you use to determine the essential elements of your "ideal" school and classroom?

3. What issues and forces do you consider to be the most troublesome ones you will face as a teacher? To what extent were they similar to or different from those of your classmates?

4. How will the No Child Left Behind legislation affect you as a teacher? How did it affect you (if at all) as a K–12 or college student?

5. How might you use the activities in this chapter to help you adjust to the school in which you do your practice teaching? How might they help you in selecting the school districts where you will seek your first teaching job? In judging your children's school as a parent?

6. How can schools encourage teachers to continue to develop as professionals? How should colleges be involved in this process?

References

Berson, M. J., and Berson, I. R. (1999, Summer). Lessons of Columbine High. *Kappa Delta Pi Record, 35(4),* 173–175.

Chiarelott, L. (2006). *Curriculum in context* (pp. 88, 112). Belmont, CA: Thomson/Wadsworth.

De Mar, G. (1997, April). *Behaviorism.* Retrieved November 9, 2002, from http://forerunner. com/forerunner/XO 4497_Demar_-Behaviorism.html.

Eisner, E. (1979). *The educational imagination: On the design and evaluation of school programs.* New York: Macmillan.

Gillespie, N. (2005, August 23). Connecticut challenges No Child Left Behind law. Associated Press. Retrieved August 25, 2005, from http://news.yahoo.com/s/ap/20050823/ap_on_re_us/ no_child_lawsuit_12.

Good, T., and Brophy, J. (1973). *Looking in classrooms.* New York: Harper & Row.

Henriques, L. (2002, May). *Constructivist teaching and learning.* Retrieved December 9, 2003, from http://www.edu.uvic.ca/depts/snsc/temporary/cnstrct.htm.

Hyman, I., and Perone, D. (1998). The other side of school violence: Educator policies and practices that may contribute to student misbehavior. *Journal of Psychology, 36(1),* 7–27.

Jencks, C. L., Smith, M., Acland, H., Bane, M. S., Cohen, D. K., Gintis, H., Heyns, B. L., and Michaelson, S. (1972). *Inequality: A reassessment of the effects of family and schooling in America.* New York: Basic Books.

Metcalf-Turner, P., and Fischetti, J. (1996, September–October). Professional development schools: Persisting questions and lessons learned. *Journal of Teacher Education,* 292–299.

National Foundation for the Improvement of Education. (1996). *Teachers take charge of their learning: Transforming professional development for student success* (p. xv). Washington, DC.

Ohio school funding: Background information. (2003, February 17). Retrieved from http:// www.ohioschoolfunding.org/background_info/background.asp.

Raywid, M. A., and Oshiyama, L. (2000, February). Musings in the wake of Columbine: What can schools do? *Phi Delta Kappan, 81(6),* 444–446, 448–449.

Rosenthal, R., and Jacobson, L. (1968). *Pygmalion in the classroom: Teacher expectation and pupils' intellectual development.* New York: Holt, Rinehart and Winston.

Sandham, J. (2001, May 2). Challenges to charter laws mount. *Education Week,* 33.

Schnaiberg, L. (1997, July 9). Ohio carves out funding for charter school pilot program. *Education Week,* 17.

Sizer, T. R. (1984). *Horace's compromise: The dilemma of the American high school.* Boston: Houghton Mifflin.

Suit alleges University of California practices religious bias. (2005, August 28). *The Toledo Blade,* 3.

Verstegen, D. A. (1994, November). The new wave of school finance litigation. *Phi Delta Kappan, 76,* 243–250.

White, K. A. (1997, June 11). Finance battles show solutions remain elusive. *Education Week, 16,* 1, 31.

Chapter 4

OBSERVING AND ANALYZING
CLASSROOM INTERACTIONS

If you are an undergraduate or graduate student considering or pursuing a career in P–12 education, there is a good chance that the framework of assessments that will lead you step-by-step to your teaching credential will involve, overlap, or be strongly influenced by a widely employed (in the United States) assessment system known as *Praxis III: Classroom Performance Assessments for Beginning Teachers*. Praxis III, developed and administered by the Educational Testing Service (ETS), is a system for assessing the skills of beginning teachers in their own classrooms, and is used by state credentialing agencies to help decide when and if a credential candidate will receive a license to teach in a given state.

The nineteen Praxis III criteria that inform the licensing decisions of credentialing agencies fall into four broad domains: (1) organizing content knowledge for student learning; (2) creating an environment for student learning; (3) teaching for student learning; and (4) teacher professionalism.* Reading and discussing the nineteen criteria will help you see that all of the recommended activities in this chapter—indeed all of the activities in this text—connect to one or more of the Praxis III criteria. Thus, in a specific way, the activities in this chapter and text are not only helping you explore the fit between yourself and a career in teaching; they are giving you knowledge and skills pertinent to what might be your ultimate goal, namely licensure.

With this in mind, we list here the nineteen Praxis III criteria, and then provide an example to illustrate how the chapter activities provide experiences, knowledge, and skills pertinent for smooth sailing through the assessment framework in place at your college or university.

THE FOUR DOMAINS AND NINETEEN CRITERIA

DOMAIN A: Organizing Content Knowledge for Student Learning

Criterion A1: Becoming familiar with relevant aspects of students' background knowledge and experiences.

---

*It is noteworthy that there is significant overlap between the Praxis III domains and the domains that are part of the California Standards for the Teaching Profession. The latter are used by mentors to guide the professional development of new teachers during their induction years program (typically their first and second years of teaching).

Criterion A2: Articulating clear learning goals for the lessons that are appropriate to the students.

Criterion A3: Demonstrating an understanding of the connections between the content that was learned previously, the current content, and the content that remains to be learned in the future.

Criterion A4: Creating or selecting teaching methods, learning activities, and instructional materials or other resources that are appropriate to the students and that are aligned with the goals of the lesson.

Criterion A5: Creating or selecting evaluation strategies that are appropriate for the students and that are aligned with the goals of the lesson.

DOMAIN B: Creating an Environment for Student Learning

Criterion B1: Creating a climate that promotes fairness.

Criterion B2: Establishing and maintaining rapport with students.

Criterion B3: Communicating challenging learning expectations to each student.

Criterion B4: Establishing and maintaining consistent standards of classroom behavior.

Criterion B5: Making the physical environment as safe and conducive to learning as possible.

DOMAIN C: Teaching for Student Learning

Criterion C1: Making learning goals and instructional procedures clear to students.

Criterion C2: Making content comprehensible to students.

Criterion C3: Encouraging students to extend their thinking.

Criterion C4: Monitoring students' understanding of content through a variety of means, providing feedback to students to assist learning, and adjusting learning activities as the situation demands.

Criterion C5: Using instructional time effectively.

DOMAIN D: Teacher Professionalism

Criterion D1: Reflecting on the extent to which the learning goals were met.

Criterion D2: Demonstrating a sense of efficacy.

Criterion D3: Building professional relationships with colleagues to share teaching insights and to coordinate learning activities for students.

Criterion D4: Communicating with parents or guardians about student learning. (Educational Testing Service, 1995)

Now for the example: In Suggested Activity 8 in this chapter you will be introduced to an elementary-oriented teacher-made survey titled "All about You." As you complete this activity, you will develop knowledge and skills that pertain to the following Praxis III criteria:

1. Becoming familiar with relevant aspects of students' background knowledge and experiences (A1).

2. Establishing and maintaining rapport with students (B2).

3. Communicating with parents and guardians about student learning (D4).

To further reinforce the linkages between the Praxis III criteria and this chapter's activities, as we introduce the Core Activity and a set of recommended related activities, we will clarify the connection between each activity and the most relevant Praxis III criteria.

Let us now turn to this chapter's Core Activity, the set of related activities, and the major difference between this chapter and the ones that preceded it. In Chapters 2 and 3 we placed you into the context of a specific school and classroom and had you focus primarily on the physical and noninteractive dimensions of school and classroom phenomena: seating arrangements, a description of a teacher's day, the location of various types of resource rooms, and so on. In this chapter the observing becomes a bit more challenging as we focus your attention on various dynamic and interactive aspects of classroom life, as well as the values, beliefs, and interests of the students you are observing. A wide range of interactions occurs daily between teachers and students, and from this wide range we have selected a set of interactions that meshes neatly with the main objective of this chapter.

In this chapter we put you in touch with the major elements of the contemporary teacher's day and role—namely lesson planning, lesson implementation (teaching), classroom management, and the ongoing study of students—and we do so in a manner that sharpens your classroom observational skills. Planning, teaching, and evaluating lessons, and then applying what you have learned, are the basic stuff of a teacher's career; and to aspire to become a teacher suggests that you want to be deeply involved with these quintessential teacher tasks. To help you be sure that this is the case, our Core Activity will give you the opportunity to observe lessons taught by experienced teachers.

Beyond the Core Activity, we offer eight carefully conceived activities that cover a wide range of interactive classroom situations. Each of these activities will make a slightly different contribution to your overall awareness of the interactive nature of teaching and the complex nature of the classroom teacher's role. The Suggested Activities will place you into a position to code various forms of praise as they occur within several lessons; to classify different types of questions; and to observe transition periods, classroom management, learning climates, cooperative learning, and the use of technology in the classroom. Although each activity in this chapter has its own introduction, a general suggestion pertaining to teacher expectations may enrich the observations that occur in several of these activities.

Since the 1960s evidence has suggested that teachers' beliefs about certain categories of students (low achievers, slow learners, etc.) help shape teachers' expectations about the learning potential of students who are placed into these socially constructed categories. These expectations, in turn, influence how teachers interact with these students. When teachers' expectations for student achievement are inaccurate, it is quite likely that inappropriate teacher–student interaction will result. Specifically, the students on the low end of the expectation continuum could receive less opportunity to respond to higher-level questioning, receive individual help and praise, have the teacher listen patiently to their responses, and so on (Brophy, 1983; Good, 1987). In educational literature, the phenomenon of teacher beliefs leading to behaviors that create classroom realities that correspond to the original beliefs is called the *self-fulfilling prophecy*. Although the evidence that has accrued regarding the self-fulfilling prophecy has been interpreted differently by some academics (Rist, 1987; Wineburg, 1987), many P-12 practitioners and teacher educators accept the proposition that what teachers believe about the learning potential of individual students, or specific groups of students such as black boys, is significant (Varlas, 2005, p. 2).

For the purpose of maximizing your observation opportunities in this chapter, as you carry out specific observational tasks, you should also watch for differential patterns of teacher praise, teacher listening, teacher questioning, teacher touching, and teacher proximity (getting close to students). As you discuss your data and impressions with fellow students, you may find that the patterns associated with negative self-fulfilling prophecies appear to be alive and well in certain classrooms. This, in turn, may lead to inquiries regarding staff development programs that aim to countervail the tendency toward negative self-fulfilling prophecies. If this occurs, a program worthy of your attention is called Teacher Expectations and Student Achievement (TESA). Between 1971 and 2006 educators representing approximately 4,800 educational agencies across the United States received TESA training. More information about TESA can be obtained by writing to TESA Program Director, Los Angeles County Office of Education, 9300 Imperial Highway, Downey, CA 90242-2890. The current TESA program director can also be reached by phone at 800-566-6651 and via e-mail at tesa_pesa@lacoe.edu. With this information shared, let us now turn to the Core Activity.

ACTIVITIES FOR CHAPTER 4

The Core Activity (Lesson Observation)

As a prospective teacher you should appreciate that if you enter the teaching profession, you will plan and teach thousands of lessons during your career. In addition, a significant portion of the teacher education program that prepares you for your career will be devoted to teaching you how to plan, implement, and evaluate lessons. This is logical: Planning and teaching lessons comprise at least two-thirds of the real work of teaching. As such they are critical activities for prospective teachers to observe and contemplate. When professionals state that teaching is hard work, they typically have in mind the detailed thinking that precedes many lessons and the large amounts of energy needed to enthusiastically deliver from six to ten lessons a day.

Because of the fundamental importance of lesson planning and implementation, in this activity you will have the opportunity to observe a variety of lessons taught by an experienced teacher or teachers; the number of lessons you observe will depend on the amount of time you have available and the length of the lesson(s) you observe.

The Observation Task(s)

The Core Activity features a lesson observation form. Your task is to (1) observe an experienced teacher as she or he teaches one or more lessons, (2) take notes while you observe, and then (3) answer as many questions as possible on the lesson observation form. As you fill in the observation form, you will note that a number of the questions tie into the effective schools information shared earlier, as well as several of the criteria in Domain C of Praxis III (e.g., makes content comprehensible to students and uses instructional time effectively).

Core Activity
LESSON OBSERVATION FORM

Your Name: _____ Participating Teacher: _____

Date: _____ Grade/Subject: _____ School: _____

1. At the beginning of the lesson, did the teacher do anything to increase the students' chances for success in this lesson? If so, please describe.

   _____

   _____

   _____

   _____

2. At the beginning of, or sometime during, the lesson, did the teacher do something to get the students interested in the lesson that they were about to experience or were experiencing? If so, please describe.

   _____

   _____

   _____

   _____

3. What was the teacher's main instructional objective in this lesson—the skill or knowledge that he or she was most interested in having the students learn (sometimes called the primary learning)?

   _____

   _____

   _____

   _____

4. What did the students learn in this lesson? You may comment here on secondary as well as primary learning.

   _____

   _____

   _____

   _____

5. What were the students' reactions to the lesson? (Observe the class as a whole as well as two specific students.)

   a. The whole class: _____

   _____

   _____

   b. The two students: _____

   _____

   _____

6. Did the teacher in any way differentiate (modify) instruction for specific students? If so, please describe.

   _____

   _____

   _____

   _____

7. In what specific ways did the teacher either praise the students or communicate high expectations to them?

   _____

   _____

   _____

   _____

8. During the lesson, did the students have the opportunity to interact with each other in dyads, triads, or in larger groups? If so, what did they do, and what do you suppose was the purpose of the student-to-student interaction?

   _____

   _____

   _____

   _____

9. Did questions asked by the teacher appear to play an important role in this lesson? If so, what were some of the pivotal questions?

   _____

   _____

_____

_____

10. What were some of the materials or visual aids that the teacher used during the lesson (examples: chalkboard, posters, pictures, audiotapes or videotapes, movies, computers)?

_____

_____

_____

11. How exactly did the teacher close the lesson?

_____

_____

_____

12. What evidence did you see that suggested that the main instructional objective of this lesson had been achieved?

_____

_____

_____

_____

13. What did you like about the way that this lesson was taught?

_____

_____

_____

_____

14. If you were going to teach this lesson to a similar group of students, what, if anything, would you change in the way that this lesson was taught, and for what reason(s)?

_____

_____

_____

_____

15. What questions do you have about the way that the lesson was presented?

_____

_____

_____

_____

_____

If you were able to speak to the teacher after the lesson, answer the following questions:

1. Was this lesson one that introduced new material, or was it a review lesson?

_____

_____

_____

_____

2. Did the teacher have a written lesson plan or some type of written notes to guide his or her instruction during the lesson? If so, please describe the written notes. Were they in a lesson plan book, on a separate sheet of paper in a lesson plan format, on an index card, or in some other form?

_____

_____

_____

_____

3. From where did the content for this lesson come?
   ❑ Teacher's original research/lesson design.   ❑ The Internet.
   ❑ A curriculum guide.   ❑ One or more of these.
   ❑ A textbook.

Suggested Activity 1

TEACHER–STUDENT INTERACTION

Increasingly, pre- and in-service teachers are being asked to play a role in the professional development of another student teacher or in-service teacher. Sometimes this new "staff development" role involves observing a live or videotaped teaching episode. Suggested Activity 1 provides a simple, flexible observation instrument that will place you into a position to collect and communicate useful data about teacher–student interaction in various types of lessons.

We have designed two different observation forms for use in classrooms with different seating arrangements. Observation Form 2 is blank because some of you may have to draw up your own seating chart to complete this activity. In addition, although in our task each symbol equals a specific teacher behavior, you can modify the symbol system to focus on other teacher behaviors. For example, the minus sign (−) could stand for students who call out an answer without raising their hands, or it could stand for students who answer questions; a plus sign (+) could stand for students who answer questions and receive praise. In a similar vein, this seating chart and symbol system could be used to compare the amount of teacher praise (or other attention) that was received by boys versus girls during a lesson.

THE TASK

Arrange to observe a teacher or student teacher who is teaching a large-group (whole-class) lesson in mathematics, social studies, English, or a similar core subject, and then follow the instructions listed here. Use Observation Form 1 or 2 to collect your data.

INSTRUCTIONS FOR USING THE TEACHER–STUDENT INTERACTION OBSERVATION FORM

1. Observe the first twenty to thirty minutes of a particular lesson.
2. Familiarize yourself with the symbols listed next and with where to place the symbols in the seating chart:
   a. The dots go into the appropriate student's Box 1. Put a dot in this box when the teacher has given the student a chance to
      (1) Answer a question.
      (2) Give a report.
      (3) Receive help from the teacher.
   b. The minus (−) signs go into Box 2. Put a minus sign in Box 2 when the teacher requests or demands that a specific child stop doing something. (This is often referred to as a *desist*.)
   c. The plus signs (+) go into Box 3. Put a plus sign in Box 3 when a student receives praise that is related to managing his or her behavior.
   d. The checks (√) go into Box 4. Put a check in Box 4 when a student receives praise for instruction-related work.

3. Occasionally the teacher will give the entire class or a specific group praise or the opportunity to respond as an entire group. Use the boxes below the seating chart to record these whole-class or small-group behaviors.
   a. Put an *X* in the "opportunity for total class response" box when the teacher asks for a total class response.
   b. Put an *X* in the "entire class receives praise" box when this occurs.
4. On the seating chart, signify whether a boy or a girl is seated there by putting a *B* or a *G* above the box. Later this will let you analyze the data in terms of gender, if you wish to do that. Other letters, of course, can indicate other identity characteristics such as language status (first or second language learners) if you are interested in coding and quantifying some other aspect of classroom interaction.
5. Fill out the comments portion of the Interaction Observation Form.

TEACHER-STUDENT INTERACTION OBSERVATION FORM 1

Teacher's Name: _____   Lesson Began: _____

Observer's Name: _____   Lesson Ended: _____

Date: _____   Lesson Content: _____
                                                    (Math, reading, etc.)

(Front of Room)

Row 1	Row 2	Row 3	Row 4	Row 5	Row 6	Row 7

(Box #)

1	2
3	4

Opportunity for total class   Entire Class Receives
Response (X)   Praise (X)

The Code:
- • = Student has opportunity to answer question, give a report, or receive help from the teacher (Box 1).
- − = Teacher asks student to stop doing something (Box 2).
- + = Student receives praise related to managing his or her behavior (Box 3).
- √ = Student receives praise that reinforces instruction (Box 4).

TEACHER–STUDENT INTERACTION OBSERVATION FORM 2

Teacher's Name: _____   Lesson Began: _____

Observer's Name: _____   Lesson Ended: _____

Date: _____   Lesson Content: _____
                                                  (Math, reading, etc.)

(Front of Room)

(Box #)

1	2
3	4

Opportunity for total class   Entire Class Receives
Response (X)   Praise (X)

The Code:
- • = Student has opportunity to answer question, give a report, or receive help from the teacher (Box 1).
- − = Teacher asks student to stop doing something (Box 2).
- + = Student receives praise related to managing his or her behavior (Box 3).
- √ = Student receives praise that reinforces instruction (Box 4).

Observer's Name: _____ Date: _____

1. Comments about the distribution of opportunity to respond, desist, or receive praise during the lesson:

_____

_____

_____

_____

_____

_____

_____

_____

2. Assuming that you were the principal of the school or this student teacher's college supervisor, what questions might you ask the teacher or student teacher if you had observed three lessons by this teacher and recorded interaction patterns similar to those that you observed today?

_____

_____

_____

_____

_____

_____

_____

_____

Suggested Activity 2

TRANSITION PERIODS

It is appropriate to draw your attention to classroom lessons and to the management problems that sometimes occur during lessons. But to more fully show you the responsibilities of a classroom teacher, an observational activity related to transitional periods—the times before, after, and between lessons and other organized activities—is also appropriate. The questions and check-off items on the Transition Period Observation Form will clarify that (1) there is more to teaching than lesson planning, implementation, and evaluation and (2) the organizational aspects of transition periods are worthy of your consideration. Indeed, time saved during a transition routine or period can be used to provide greater amounts of academic learning time for students. Parenthetically, the skills associated with developing efficient transition routines pertain to specific Domain B and C criteria in Praxis III (e.g., make the physical environment as safe and conducive to learning as possible).

Before you use the Transition Period Observation Form, some examples of transition period times and activities should prove helpful. For example, during the elementary school day, between lessons, you might see a teacher walk her class out to the playground for a physical education activity or to the bathroom; you might also see the students given a few minutes of free (decision-making) time or some time to organize their homework packets to take home or to set up for the teacher's inspection. In a similar vein, you might see an elementary, junior high, or high school teacher taking roll, checking homework, lining students up for dismissal or lunch, or simply telling students to turn to a specific page in a textbook and then to look up when they are ready for the next lesson.

Use the Transition Period Observation Form on the same days that you carry out your Core Activity or Suggested Activity 1 to observe how teachers manage time during transition periods. This form can be used for observation at any time of the day because lessons are always beginning and ending with transitions occurring before and after. It is noteworthy that research has revealed that teachers vary widely in their ability to efficiently organize their transition periods.

TRANSITION PERIOD OBSERVATION FORM*

Your Name: _____ Participating Teacher: _____

Date: _____ Grade/Subject: _____ School: _____

1. During the transition or routine does the teacher do things that students could do for themselves?

   _____

   _____

   _____

2. Does the teacher give clear instructions about what to do next before moving into a transition period?

   _____

   _____

   _____

3. Is the transition period routine (taking attendance, lining up to sharpen pencils, moving to another seating arrangement, etc.) organized in a time-efficient manner, or can a more time-efficient routine be developed?

   _____

   _____

   _____

4. Does the teacher circulate during transitions to handle individual needs? Does he or she take care of these before attempting to begin a new activity?

   _____

   _____

   _____

5. Does the teacher signal the end of a transition and the beginning of a structured activity properly and quickly gain everyone's attention?

   _____

   _____

   _____

---

*Adaptation of two forms from *Looking in Classrooms* (4th ed.) by T. L. Good and J. E. Brophy, 1987, Harper & Row. Reprinted by permission of the publisher.

6. Does the teacher use singing, background music, or any other creative device to add spice to the transition period/routine?

_____

_____

_____

Check if applicable:

_____ 1. Transitions occur too abruptly for students because the teacher fails to give advance warning or finish-up reminders when needed.

_____ 2. The teacher insists on unnecessary rituals or formalisms that cause delays or disruptions.

_____ 3. The teacher is interrupted by individuals with the same problem or request; this could be handled by establishing a general rule or procedure (describe).

_____

_____

_____

_____ 4. Delays occur because frequently used materials are stored in hard-to-reach places.

_____ 5. Poor traffic patterns result in pushing, bumping, or unnecessary noise.

_____ 6. Delays occur while the teacher prepares equipment or illustrates what should have been prepared earlier.

_____ 7. Behavioral problems occur because of lack of structure during transition or because of other unidentified reasons.

Suggested Activity 3
CLASSROOM MANAGEMENT

Classroom management and effective teaching are like inhaling and exhaling. They are inextricably intertwined, part of an ongoing process, but are often considered and discussed as separate processes. Indeed, for most teachers the words *classroom management* and *teaching* point to different areas of a teacher's responsibilities. Further, university-level teacher education programs often feature a specific course on classroom management and several courses on instruction of one kind or another. The classroom management course is considered critical and will usually contain readings, lectures, and discussions about how to create and maintain good student behavior; arrange your classroom to promote effective instruction; get off to a good start at the beginning of the year; and organize and manage the flow of information and paper that occurs before, during, and after instruction. Classroom management, in short, is about all the little and big things (tactics and strategies) that teachers do to create an environment in which learning occurs smoothly and efficiently for a wide range of learners. Note that classroom management knowledge and skills are well represented among the Praxis III criteria (e.g., establish and maintain consistent standards of classroom behavior and create a climate that promotes fairness).

In recent years educational research has validated a number of logical ideas about classroom management. For example, regarding good room arrangement, student teachers are taught to keep high-traffic areas free of congestion, be sure that all students are easily seen by the teacher, and be sure that all students can easily see instructional presentations. In a related vein, a consensus has grown around the use of rules in both elementary and secondary settings. Today student teachers are taught how to develop a set of rules with their students and are usually told to keep the number of rules to somewhere between five and eight.

Although education research has provided a set of validated tactics and strategies for classroom management, teachers will always encounter behavioral situations that require special data collection, thought, and solutions. Some exposure to these types of problems will show why the teaching profession needs bright people who can collect and analyze data that are unique to a situation to come up with a variety of possible solutions and a plan of action.

The three observation forms provided in Suggested Activity 3 will allow you to observe classroom management from several vantage points. These forms can be used individually or together. For example, you might start with Form A and note that a particular student presents a significant behavior problem. In some elementary and in most secondary settings you might then choose to observe this same student in one or more different classrooms. Form B, which focuses on the effects that different teachers have on the same student, may prove helpful here, particularly if you are in a secondary school setting. Form C, which focuses on off-task and on-task behavior, is another good source of case study data. Note that the observation activities focus on the student behavior aspect of classroom management. As indicated, classroom management is concerned with a wide-ranging set of classroom conditions and factors, all of which influence student behavior and learning. As you observe and interview in the activities in various chapters throughout this text and beyond, you'll find it helpful to maintain an active curiosity about classroom management.

You can begin this activity with Form A and observe in three or four classrooms before choosing to use Forms B and C. Or you might start with Form A and use that form for all of your observations.

CLASSROOM MANAGEMENT OBSERVATION FORM A

Your Name: _____ Participating Teacher: _____

Date: _____ Grade/Subject: _____ School: _____

Focus: Classroom management in one classroom.

Data Collection

1. Did you notice any behavioral problems in this classroom? If so, please describe.

   _____

   _____

   _____

   _____

2. How did the teacher respond to these problems?

   _____

   _____

   _____

   _____

3. What was the student's or students' immediate response to the teacher's response to the misbehavior?

   _____

   _____

   _____

   _____

4. During the lesson did the teacher make positive statements to the whole class and/or to individual students to reward and encourage appropriate behavior? If so, describe some of these positive statements.

   _____

   _____

   _____

   _____

5. Did the teacher use what you would consider to be negative measures in response to student misbehavior? If so, describe these measures.

_____

_____

_____

_____

_____

6. What classroom routines were utilized during this lesson, if any? Describe the routines if they were present, and speculate about whether the routines worked for or against establishing a positive environment for learning.

_____

_____

_____

_____

Analysis

1. During this observation period, which management techniques appeared to be most effective?

_____

_____

_____

_____

2. Which techniques, if any, appeared problematic or ineffective to you? What questions do you have about these techniques?

_____

_____

_____

_____

_____

CLASSROOM MANAGEMENT OBSERVATION FORM B

Your Name: _____ Participating Teacher: _____

Date: _____ Grade/Subject: _____ School: _____

Focus: The behavior of one student in several classrooms.

Data Collection

Observe one student's reactions in two or three different classes, noting his or her participation, facial expressions, body language, involvement in class, and relationships with peers and teachers.

1. How are these classrooms alike, and how are they different?

   _____

   _____

   _____

   _____

2. Is the mix of students roughly the same in all the classes? If not, how are the classes different?

   _____

   _____

   _____

   _____

3. Does the student's behavior change from class to class? If so, describe the change.

   _____

   _____

   _____

   _____

4. Does the change in behavior, either positive or negative, appear to be triggered by specific teacher behaviors? If so, what teacher behaviors appear to be associated with the change in student behavior?

   _____

   _____

   _____

   _____

5. Is there any chance that your student's behavior change might be linked to the subject matter being taught? If so, why do you think this *might* be the case?

_____

_____

_____

_____

6. Are there any other possible explanations for the student's behavior? If so, please spell out competing explanations that *might* be involved.

_____

_____

_____

_____

7. What do different teachers do to encourage effective communication with the student you are observing as well as with other students?

_____

_____

_____

_____

_____

_____

_____

_____

8. What do you see teachers doing that appears to inhibit effective communication?

_____

_____

_____

_____

_____

_____

_____

_____

_____

_____

Analysis

If you were a school counselor providing suggestions to all of the teachers with whom this student interacted, what suggestions might you provide?

_____

_____

_____

_____

_____

_____

_____

_____

_____

_____

CLASSROOM MANAGEMENT OBSERVATION FORM C

Your Name: _____   Participating Teacher: _____

Date: _____   Grade/Subject: _____   School: _____

First Name of Observed Student: _____

Focus: Measuring individual students' academic engaged time by recording students' on-task and off-task behavior.

Data Collection

Identify the student(s) whom you intend to observe before the observation day. Observe the first student on your list; if that student is absent, observe the second student on your list. Observe each student for thirty minutes during a lesson. At the end of each minute during the lesson, observe the student and mark the choice here that best describes the student's behavior. When finished, you will have recorded thirty observations. When the thirty-minute observation period is completed, add up the checks in each row, total the on-task and off-task behavior, and then work out the percentages for on-task and off-task behavior.

ON-TASK BEHAVIOR

The student is engaged in tasks related to academic material. These may include listening to the teacher, asking questions, completing an assignment, and so on.

Record Checks Here

☐ = Total number of checks for on-task behavior   ☐ = % On-task academic behavior*

OFF-TASK BEHAVIOR

Record Checks Here

1. Daydreaming _____

2. Socializing _____

3. Doodling _____

4. Playing with other students _____

5. Misbehaving generally _____

6. Waiting for assistance _____

7. Sharpening pencil _____

8. Getting materials needed for lesson _____

9. Getting a drink of water _____

10. Leaving to go to the bathroom _____

11. Being interrupted or distracted from lesson by an intercom message, fire drill, another student, and so on _____

☐ = Total number of checks for on-task behavior   ☐ = % On-task academic behavior*

---

*For example, if there were ten checks for on-task behavior and twenty checks for off-task behavior, the respective percentages would be 33 percent and 67 percent. Roughly speaking, one could say that this student had a 33 percent academic-engaged rate during this lesson.

Suggested Activity 4
CLASSROOM ARRANGEMENT

The working, teaching, and learning environments that teachers create for students vary greatly across grades and within grades. To gain insight into the physical as well as the instructional dimensions and implications of this range, complete one or more of the following tasks:

1. Gain permission to visit many classrooms in a single school. Spend approximately ten to fifteen minutes in each classroom taking general notes about bulletin boards, file cabinets, chalkboard space, seating arrangements, aesthetic appeal, and so on. Spend the bulk of your time in the classroom just looking and trying to get a feel for the atmosphere and/or the learning climate.

2. After you have visited a large number of classrooms, compare and contrast three or more of the classrooms that you thought had interesting designs.

3. Arrange to observe a lesson in a room that you felt was well organized and tastefully arranged. Arrange to observe a lesson in a classroom that was poorly organized and less tastefully arranged. Use the lesson observation form from the Core Activity to collect data on the lessons. After data collection, compare and contrast the two lessons. Was there any relationship between the quality of classroom design and the quality of lesson design and implementation?

Finally, note that this activity provides knowledge that pertains to Domain B of Praxis III (creating an environment for student learning), and more specifically this criterion: "makes the physical environment as safe and conducive to learning as possible."

Suggested Activity 5
QUESTIONING

To help you gain a well-rounded view of the career that you are considering, we have encouraged you to observe as much teaching as possible because planning and implementing lessons are fundamental and pervasive dimensions of teaching. We will now help you take a closer look at a significant component of lesson planning and lesson execution—question creation and questioning itself.

The development of patterns of questions that have appropriate variety, as well as single questions that are intriguing and original, is a satisfying aspect of teaching. However, research has consistently demonstrated that many teachers deliver patterns or sets of questions that are predominantly lower-order—that is, questions that deal with memorization and factual recall of information. These memory-level questions do not require students to do something challenging with the retrieved information (e.g., interpret, analyze, compare and contrast, synthesize, evaluate, create). Interestingly, some education writers have argued that effective teaching for certain groups of students will involve high percentages of factual, lower-order questions. At the same time, the wisdom of teaching (accumulated practical experience) indicates that most students benefit from judicious mixtures of higher-order and lower-order questions, as well as the opportunity to develop and answer their own interesting questions.

The forms utilized in this activity will introduce you to a tool for determining the percentage of lower-order and higher-order questions asked by teacher and students in a selected lesson, as well as the teacher's questioning rate (the number of questions asked per minute). If you proceed into the final phases of a teacher preparation program, you can use this tool to work out the ratio of higher- to lower-order questions in your own (tape-recorded) lessons.

The second part of this activity will help you observe the effects of "teacher wait time" on the level of oral participation in selected classrooms and lessons. The research base on this significant instructional variable dates back to the pioneering work of Mary Budd Rowe (1974) in the early 1970s. Rowe contended that slowing down the pace of question-and-answer classroom communication would have a variety of positive results, and research conducted in the mid-1980s supported her claim (Tobin, 1986, 1987). When students are given more time to think after a question is asked, more students are able to respond, the length of their remarks increases, and the students are more likely to listen and respond to each other. A good deal of research has shown that many teachers, after asking a question, wait less than a second before rephrasing the question, answering it themselves, or asking another question. Research also suggests that many teachers, for a variety of reasons, favor boys over girls when it comes to the opportunity to ask and answer questions across the curriculum and in specific content areas (Campbell, 1986; Sadker and Sadker, 1986; American Association of University Women, 1992). As noted earlier, Teacher–Student Interaction Form 1 can be used to see if gender-defined patterns of behavior are manifested in the classes that you are observing. In addition, staff development efforts in this area have attempted to train teachers to expand their wait time to three or more seconds between the question and the next teacher move, and also to eliminate gender bias. It is noteworthy that the research literature on wait time presents findings regarding *wait time one* and *wait time two*: After the teacher calls on someone to answer a question, the latter refers to how long the teacher waits before calling on another student, answering the question herself, or asking a new question (Good and Brophy, 2003, p. 383; Marzano, Pickering, and Pollack, 2001, p. 114). It will be interesting to see the results from your own observation in this area. You might find it illuminating to observe the style and pattern of questioning in a classroom without any predetermined focus to see where an open-minded, open-ended observation might lead. To facilitate this observation, we have included the Qualitative Questioning Observation Form. Finally, a perusal of Domain C of Praxis III will reveal that skill in formulating and asking questions is linked to each of the five criteria in that domain.

HIGHER-ORDER/LOWER-ORDER QUESTIONING ANALYSIS FORM

Your Name: _____   Participating Teacher: _____

Date: _____   Grade/Subject: _____   School: _____

Focus: The ratio of lower-order to higher-order questions asked in specific lessons and the teacher's questioning rate.

Information

Lower-order questions require memorization and recall of factual information. The student does not use the information in any way (to apply, analyze, evaluate, etc.). The student is asked to retrieve certain information from her or his memory bank.

Here are some examples of lower-order questions:

1. Who was the first president of the United States?
2. Which American president went into politics after a career in acting?
3. In which American city is the White House located?
4. Yesterday we discussed the factors that led to the Civil War. Who remembers which factor was considered most important?

Higher-order questions require students to use the information recalled in some manner—such as explaining its meaning, comparing or contrasting it to something else, making a generalization, applying it to solve a problem, or analyzing, synthesizing, or evaluating the information.

Here are some examples of higher-order questions and tasks:

1. What does this poem mean to you?
2. Do you think the poet embedded a special message in the poem? If so, what is it?
3. Why do you think Ronald Reagan was such a popular president?
4. Which generalization about the factors contributing to the Civil War appears most accurate to you? Explain your choice.
5. If you pull all of this information together, which solutions to the problem emerge?

Data Collection

Nature and Number of Teacher Questions

1. Select a typical thirty-minute segment of teacher–student interaction and tape-record the teaching episode. Then enter on two sheets of paper the questions asked by the teacher and the questions asked by the students.
2. How many teacher questions were higher-order thought questions?
3. How many teacher questions were lower-order memory questions?
4. What was the percentage of higher-order questions asked by the teacher?

$$\frac{\text{Higher-order questions}}{\text{Total questions}} = \text{Percentage}$$

5. What was the rate of question asking by the teacher?

$$\frac{\text{Total questions asked}}{20 \text{ minutes}} = \text{Teacher questions per minute}$$

6. How many of the student questions were higher-order thought questions?

7. How many of the student questions were lower-order memory questions?

8. What was the percentage of higher-order questions asked by the students?

$$\frac{\text{Higher-order questions}}{\text{Total questions}} = \text{Percentage}$$

9. What was the rate of question asking by all students? What was the average rate of question asking by a single student?

$$\text{Total student rate} = \frac{\text{Total questions asked}}{20 \text{ minutes}} = \text{Total student questions per minute}$$

$$\text{Average student rate} = \frac{\text{Total student questions per minute}}{\text{Number of students in the class}}$$

Analysis

1. Compare the questioning rates and questioning ratios (higher-order to lower-order) of teacher and students in this lesson. What observations can you derive from this comparison?

_____

_____

_____

_____

2. Analyze the content, clarity, sequence, and thought-provoking quality of the teacher's questions. What observations can you derive from this analysis? Does this analysis lead to observations that are similar to or different than the observations derived from analysis of questioning rate and ratio?

_____

_____

_____

_____

3. If you were this teacher's coach or supervisor, would you have any advice to give about the questions in this lesson? If so, please spell this out.

_____

_____

_____

_____

THE TEACHER'S QUESTIONS

1. _____

2. _____

3. _____

4. _____

5. _____

6. _____

7. _____

8. _____

9. _____

10. _____

11. _____

12. _____

13. _____

14. _____

15. _____

16. _____

17. _____

18. _____

19. _____

20. _____

21. _____

22. _____

23. _____

24. _____

25. _____

THE STUDENTS' QUESTIONS

1. _____

2. _____

3. _____

4. _____

5. _____

6. _____

7. _____

8. _____

9. _____

10. _____

11. _____

12. _____

13. _____

14. _____

15. _____

16. _____

17. _____

18. _____

19. _____

20. _____

WAIT TIME IN QUESTIONING ANALYSIS FORM

Your Name: _____ Participating Teacher: _____

Date: _____ Grade/Subject: _____ School: _____

Focus: Analysis of wait time in questioning.

Information

Research has demonstrated that the number of seconds that a teacher waits after asking a question dramatically influences the range of student response in a classroom (the number of pupils who want to orally respond) and the length of individual oral responses. In this activity we focus on the teacher's wait time after he or she has asked a question. Parenthetically, a wait of three seconds is generally considered a productive amount of time, but some teachers find that their students benefit from lengthier wait times (five to ten seconds). Also, teachers often refer to this variable as *think time*.

Data Collection

Use a stopwatch and the audiotape of the teaching episode from the previous activity to answer the following questions:

1. What is the teacher's average wait time for lower-order questions?

   _____

2. What is the teacher's average wait time for higher-order questions?

   _____

3. What is the teacher's overall wait time for all questions?

   _____

4. Is the teacher's wait time for lower-order and higher-order questions generally consistent, or does she or he have a combination of short (less than a second) and long (five- to fifteen-second) wait times?

   _____

5. Do the students' responses appear to be affected by the teacher's wait time? If so, in what way(s)?

   _____

   _____

   _____

   _____

Analysis

1. What observations derive from your comparison of wait times for lower-order versus higher-order questions?

    _____

    _____

    _____

    _____

2. If you were this teacher's coach or supervisor, would you have any wait-time advice to offer? If so, spell out the advice.

    _____

    _____

    _____

    _____

3. What other factors, beyond teacher wait time, do you think might cause a wide range of students to want to give an oral response? Which of these do you consider most significant and why?

    _____

    _____

    _____

    _____

QUALITATIVE QUESTIONING OBSERVATION FORM

Your Name: _____   Participating Teacher: _____

Date: _____   Grade/Subject: _____   School: _____

Special characteristics of class (class size, demographic profile, and so on):

_____

_____

Focus: None.

Information and Directions

Much can be learned about the art of questioning simply by observing master teachers. Also, much that is pertinent regarding style in questioning does not lend itself to numerical treatment. As you observe master teachers, try to discern and to describe what makes their approach to questioning successful. Where possible, try to follow up your observation with an interview in which teachers have an opportunity to discuss their approach to question creation and delivery. Also, if you perceive a way to quantify your observations, by all means do so.

Suggested Activity 6

OBSERVATION OF COOPERATIVE LEARNING

As you progress through your teacher education program, you will have many opportunities to consider and discuss general approaches to teaching (direct, indirect, and self-directed), along with more specific approaches such as mastery learning, whole-language learning, differentiated instruction and cooperative learning, and finally a wide variety of instructional strategies associated with one or more of these approaches (lecture, discussion, role-playing, cross-age tutoring, sociodrama, sustained silent reading and writing, tableau, the seven-step "Hunter" model, bibliotherapy, and so on).

Within this complex universe of approaches and strategies, cooperative learning occupies a special niche and traverses a unique orbit. It is simultaneously an excellent instructional strategy, a highly effective tool for classroom management, and a powerful strategy for reducing prejudice and negative discrimination between boys and girls and various ethnocultural groups. Indeed, as Davidman and Davidman (2001, p. 115) note, "Research data accumulated over three decades strongly suggest that cooperative learning is a powerful cross-content, cross-grade level strategy for simultaneously accomplishing several of the goals of multicultural education, namely educational equity, intergroup understanding and harmony, and the establishment of positive, collaborative, empowering relationships between students, teachers, and parents." The conclusions reached by the Davidmans are supported by two influential educational researchers, Robert Slavin and Robert Marzano. For example, in his illuminating text on cooperative learning (1995, p. 21) Slavin wrote, "Overall, the effects of cooperative learning on achievement are clearly positive. Sixty-three (63%) of the ninety-nine experimental control comparisons significantly favored cooperative learning. Only five (5%) significantly favored control groups." Similarly, Marzano, Pickering, and Pollock, in their influential text on research-based instructional strategies (2001, p. 87), state, "In general, then, organizing students in cooperative learning groups has a powerful effect on learning, regardless of whether groups compete with one another." It is noteworthy also that Marzano and his colleagues conclude (p. 88) that "Cooperative learning should be applied consistently and systematically, but not overused." This generalization is worthy of analysis and discussion, and it is our hope that the following observation task will give you the opportunity to do so. With regard to the Praxis III assessment criteria, knowledge and skill about cooperative learning directly pertain to criteria A4 (selecting appropriate teaching methods) and B1 (creating a climate that promotes fairness).

THE OBSERVATION TASK

With the help of your instructor, identify a teacher who is noted for his or her utilization of cooperative learning methods. Arrange to observe for more than one period or lesson, and where possible,

1. Arrange to observe in a classroom where the student population is characterized by ethnic and linguistic diversity.
2. Receive permission to talk with students after the cooperative group work is completed.

3. Try to interview the teacher about his or her approach to, and experience with, co-operative learning. For example, how long has the teacher been using cooperative learning, and how did she or he get started? Has the teacher been influenced by one or more specific approaches to cooperative learning, such as those articulated by David and Roger Johnson, Elizabeth Cohen, Robert Slavin, Spencer Kagan, and/or Alfie Cohen?

COOPERATIVE LEARNING OBSERVATION FORM

Your Name: _____ Participating Teacher: _____

Date: _____ Grade/Subject: _____ School: _____

Special characteristics of class (class size, size of cooperative learning groups, demographic profile, and so on):

_____

_____

Focus: The utilization of cooperative learning.

Data Collection

1. Did this lesson have an instructional focus? If so, what do you think the teacher would identify as the main instructional objective(s)?

   a. _____

   _____

   _____

   b. _____

   _____

   _____

2. Was cooperative learning the main instructional strategy in this lesson or one of several employed? If the latter, which other strategies were employed?

   _____

   _____

   _____

3. Prior to releasing the students to work in their cooperative groups, what, if anything, did the teacher say to the students to promote effective group functioning?

   _____

   _____

   _____

4. What did the teacher do while the cooperative learning groups were functioning?

_____

_____

_____

5. Were the groups in this class during this learning activity in competition with each other? If so, what effect did this appear to have on the learning?

_____

_____

_____

6. Overall (across all groups in the class), how well did the students appear to be interacting with each other?

_____

_____

_____

7. In the one or two groups that you were closely observing,

   a. How many of the students were consistently on-task in a (seemingly) productive manner?

_____

_____

   b. Did students have the same or different responsibilities in the task, or a little bit of both?

_____

_____

8. Were the groups diversely structured in academic skills, gender, and/or ethnicity?

_____

_____

9. In the group(s) that you closely observed, did the member(s) of one cultural (girls/boys) group or ethnic (Hispanic, white, black, Asian, etc.) group appear to dominate the interaction?

_____

_____

10. Did the students in each group appear to be playing special roles at least part of the time—expert instructor, encourager, scribe, reporter, praiser, resource distributor, timekeeper, and so forth?

_____

_____

_____

11. What did you learn about classroom management from observing these lessons?

_____

_____

_____

_____

12. From your observation of these lessons, what questions would you like to ask the classroom teacher? Your course instructor?

_____

_____

_____

_____

_____

_____

Comparison, Contrast, and Analysis

1. What were the significant differences between this learning environment and other class-rooms you have recently observed?

   _____

   _____

   _____

   _____

2. Was the teacher's role (behavior) in this class different than in others you have recently observed? If so, please elaborate.

   _____

   _____

   _____

   _____

3. To the extent that you observed differences in student and teacher behavior in the cooper-ative learning environment, to what do you attribute these differences?

   _____

   _____

   _____

   _____

Suggested Activity 7

EDUCATIONAL USES OF TECHNOLOGY

In the Core Activity for this chapter we said that planning and teaching lessons comprise at least two-thirds of the real work of teaching. But in what type of classroom, and with what technology, will these lessons be created and delivered? We are all aware that traditional notions of planning, teaching, and evaluation have recently been creatively challenged, with more challenges on the horizon. Our instructional lexicon now includes terms like distance education, Web quests, electronic research tools, threaded discussions, e-mail aliases, downloadable journal articles, and much more. Thus it is fair to say that many U.S. educational environments (schools, museums, homeschool settings, etc.) are experiencing transformation, albeit in an unequal manner. What will teaching look like in this transformed future?

We believe that present-day pedagogy provides some clues. Contemporary teachers on the technological edge are already teaching to their objectives via interactive technology (televisions, tape recordings, computers, handheld devices, video cameras, digital cameras, and more). They are using presentation programs like Power-Point and handheld devices and probes for science experiments, and their students are producing videos for various purposes. In addition, many of these technology-oriented teachers are (1) utilizing their own Web pages to present content to their students and the parents or guardians of their students and (2) using the Internet to involve their students in national and international scientific inquiries.

Because of the importance of technology in the future we envision, we invite you to engage in two activities. The first is a classroom observation task similar to other observation tasks in this text. The second activity will involve you in a self-directed, unstructured examination of a set of education-oriented Web sites compiled by technology author and consultant Marsha Lifter. To facilitate this review, Lifter has divided the set of online teacher resources into three categories: sites for teachers, experiences for teachers and students, and productivity tools. For each entry she provides the site name, the Web site address, and a brief description of site contents. Let us turn now to the specifics of Suggested Activity 7.

THE OBSERVATION TASK

On your own or with the help of your professor, identify a classroom, learning laboratory, or computer lab and arrange to observe instruction in this learning environment for several hours. Where possible,

1. Arrange to conduct your observation in a setting in which the instructor has a reputation for creative use of interactive technology (computers, videotape machines, television, etc.).
2. Observe different ages of children learning in the technological learning environment.
3. Receive permission to talk with (interview) children about their learning during the class period.

TECHNOLOGY IN THE CLASSROOM OBSERVATION FORM

Your Name: _____ Participating Teacher: _____

Date: _____ Grade/Subject: _____ School: _____

Focus: The use of technology to deliver various forms of individualized instruction.

Data Collection

1. What technology was in use in this classroom or learning laboratory?

   a. _____

   _____

   b. _____

   _____

   c. _____

   _____

   d. _____

   _____

2. In what ways did the teacher interact with the students in this learning environment?

   _____

   _____

   _____

   _____

3. What activities were students engaged in within this learning environment?

   _____

   _____

   _____

   _____

4. What kinds of individual or group learning activities were students engaged in while you were observing them?

   _____

   _____

_____

_____

5. Did the classroom or learning laboratory that you were observing appear to have classroom management problems or discipline problems? If so, please describe them.

_____

_____

_____

_____

6. To what extent were the students in this classroom or learning laboratory engaged in the activity (on-task) as opposed to being off-task (in one way or another)?

_____

_____

_____

_____

7. What were students learning in this classroom or learning environment?

_____

_____

_____

_____

_____

_____

8. Were the students in this classroom or learning laboratory engaged in higher-level tasks (analyzing, interpreting, evaluating, creating, problem creating, problem solving)? If so, describe what they were doing.

_____

_____

_____

_____

_____

_____

Comparison, Contrast, and Analysis

1. What were the significant differences between this classroom or learning environment and other classrooms you have recently observed?

   _____

   _____

   _____

   _____

   _____

2. Were you excited by what you observed in this classroom or learning environment? Why or why not?

   _____

   _____

   _____

   _____

   _____

3. Does the teacher's role appear to change in this kind of learning environment? If so, how are the roles of the teacher different in this class than in other classrooms you have recently observed?

   _____

   _____

   _____

   _____

   _____

4. If students' learning behavior in this classroom or learning environment was different than that of students whom you observed in other types of classrooms, to what do you attribute this difference?

   _____

   _____

   _____

   _____

   _____

5. To what extent did the students in this classroom appear to be controlled by the technology, as opposed to being in a position to use the technology to have control over their learning process?

_____

_____

_____

_____

_____

6. To what extent, if any, did there appear to be gender or ethnocultural group differences in the utilization of the electronic learning tools in the lab? If you noted such differences, what might be the contributing factors?

_____

_____

_____

_____

_____

THE WEBSITE EXPLORATION TASK

As noted earlier, this task is included here as a self-directed activity. How you interact with these sites will vary according to your available time, curiosity, prior knowledge, and the point of view of your instructor.

Sites for Teachers

Lesson plans, bulletin boards, teaching ideas, activities, resources, site links, and much more can be found at the following sites:

Site name: MarcoPolo (K–12)
Named after the explorer, this site links educators to whatever they are exploring for. An excellent place to start your journey.
www.marcopolo.org

Site name: Teaching Ideas for Primary Teachers (K–3)
Easy-to-follow listing of new ideas in all subject areas—even rather abstract subjects like "time fillers." You can share your ideas.
http://www.teachingideas.co.uk/

Site name: Pro Teacher! (K–12)
This site is a must for new teachers. It is a posting site for teacher ideas in the area of classroom management and gives great ideas for class meetings.
http://www.proteacher.com/030000.shtml

Site name: Resources for Elementary Teachers (K–6)
Links to excellent sites for teachers and students.
http://www.salem.k12.va.us/south/teacher/

Site name: Four Great Teacher Spots (K–6)
Provides a link for first-year teachers. Lesson plans, advice, ideas, you name it—they've got it.
http://www.theteacherspot.com/

Site name: Crayola (Pre-K–6)
Incorporates art and writing lessons in all curriculum areas.
www.crayola.com/educators/lessons

Site name: Lesson Planz.com (K–6)
This site has lesson plans for all grades along with some great poems and songs.
http://lessonplanz.com

Site name: Learningpage (K–6)
Lesson plans on animals, math, science, vocabulary, reading, worksheets; requires registration.
www.learningpage.com/free

Site name: Physical Education Lesson Plans (K–12)
Physical education integrated into academic lesson plans.
www.members.tripod.com/~pazz/lesson.html

Site name: Blue Web (K–12)
Web education activities including Web quests.
www.bluewebn.com

Site name: Ed Helper (K–8)
Lesson plans, Web quests, worksheets, sites.
www.edhelper.com

Site name: Educate the Children
Ideas for activities for teachers and parents to demonstrate concepts.
http://www.exploratorium.edu/science

Site name: Enchanted Learning Software (K–6)
Literature-based lesson plans. Choose a subject and get lessons. Lists appropriate grade level activity sheets.
www.enchantedlearning.com

Site name: A–Z Teacher Stuff (K–12)
Activities for particular holidays and seasons grouped by themes. Also has chat rooms for teachers.
http://www.atozteacherstuff.com

Site name: Discovery School.com (K–12)
Lesson plans for all grades; create and customize worksheets and puzzles for activities. Has clip art that can be downloaded.
http://school.discovery.com/schoolhome.html

Site name: Teachnet.com (K–6)
Lesson plans for all ages and grade levels. Has bulletin boards where teachers can share ideas.
http://www.teachnet.com

Site name: Kiddy House (Pre-K–2)
Fabulous site for lesson plans, holiday activities.
http://www.kiddyhouse.com

Site name: Yahooligans
Yahoo's kid directory of 20,000+ sites that are kid appropriate.
www.yahooligans.com

Site name: Education World (K–12)
Resources related to practically every aspect of education.
www.educationworld.com

Site name: Arts Edge (K–12)
Great resource for incorporating performing arts and technology into regular classroom curricula.
http://artsedge.kennedy-center.org

Site name: The Teacher's Corner (K–8)
Everything you could ever want as a teacher: bulletin boards, lesson plans, resources, thematic units, and more.
http://www.theteacherscorner.net/index.htm

Site name: Bulletin Boards
Really creative ideas for bulletin boards.
http://www.kimskorner4teachertalk.com/classmanagement/bulletinboards.html

Experiences for Teachers and Students

Site name: Exploratorium
This site has many hands-on activities that relate to different aspects of science.
http://www.exploratorium.edu

Site name: Smithsonian
Provides mini-units including three to four lessons and a follow-up on different science topics.
http://educate.si.edu

Site name: Virtual Field Trips
A tour through different Web sites to learn about subjects like salt marshes or volcanoes. Includes lesson plans and teacher resources.
http://www.field-guides.com

Site name: Seaworld
Site includes lesson plans in Spanish.
www.seaworld.org

Site name: Create an Environment for a Tiger Online
www.CyberTiger@nationalgeographic.org

Productivity Tools

Site name: Cool Text
Hundreds of unique fonts for use.
http://www.cooltext.com

Site name: Kids Domain (K–6)
Clip art for fun.
www.kidsdomain.com/clip

Site name: Find Sounds
Search the Web for sounds with an easy search engine.
www.findsounds.com

Site name: Freeplay Music
Largest collection of free music available online.
www.freeplaymusic.com

Clip art for teachers:

http://school.discovery.com/clipart/
http://www.teacherfiles.com/clip_art.htm
http://www.awesomeclipartforkids.com/

Suggested Activity 8

UTILIZING A TEACHER-MADE SURVEY

The more you know about your students, the greater your potential to understand their behavior, develop long-lasting rapport, and help them experience academic success. One simple way to begin the yearlong or semesterlong self-disclosure process is to invite your students to complete a survey that you have had a chance to adapt. The "All about You" survey, which is the focus of Suggested Activity 8, was developed by an upper-grade elementary school teacher in Santa Maria, California, and it is in the public domain. Therefore, you can tinker with it to your heart's delight. But where and when will your tinkering and adaptation take place? Ideally, your work with the "All about You" survey will occur early in your field assignment in one of the classes you are observing. You will, of course, need the approval of the teacher you are observing, and it would be wise to get the principal's approval as well. When these approvals are in place, you will be ready to carry out the task delineated here.

THE SURVEY IMPLEMENTATION TASK

1. Review the questions on the survey and make revisions (add, delete, and modify) so the information collected will be appropriate for a short-term observer like yourself, as opposed to a yearlong elementary school teacher. Try to get down to ten to twelve questions.

2. Explain to the students how their survey responses will make your observations in their class more illuminating. After answering any questions students have about your "illuminating" remark, discuss the term "confidentiality." Let the students know that the information they share will be considered confidential, and explain how you will accomplish this.

3. Make it clear to students that filling out the survey is purely voluntary. It is not required, and if they choose to participate they don't have to answer each question. Tell the students that you will read each question to the class.

4. Administer the survey, analyze your data, and write a preliminary report that summarizes what you have learned from your data analysis. Later in your assignment, revise the preliminary report to include material that responds to the following questions:
   a. Did the survey information make you a more insightful observer and interpreter of classroom phenomena? If so, give some examples.
   b. Did the survey information enhance your instructional relationship with one or more students in the class? If so, please specify.
   c. Did the survey process lead to any unanticipated outcomes?

ALL ABOUT YOU

1. What is your full name? _____

2. Do you have a nickname? What is it? _____

3. Who calls you by that nickname and why? _____

_____

4. When is your birthday? _____

5. How old are you? _____

6. Where were you born? _____

7. What are your address and phone number? _____

_____

8. How many brothers and sister do you have? _____

9. Who lives in your house with you? _____

_____

10. In your family, are you the oldest child, youngest child, or somewhere in the middle?

_____

11. What languages do you speak? ___ _____

12. What language do you speak at home with your family? _____

13. Do you have a pet? What kind? _____

14. What is your favorite hobby? _____

15. Whom do you like to spend time with? _____

16. Who was your teacher last year? _____

17. Have you been to any other schools besides_____ school? If so, how many? _____

18. What is your favorite thing about school? _____

_____

19. What is your favorite thing to do with your family? _____

_____

20. Tell me one or more things about yourself that you think is or are interesting:

_____

_____

_____

_____

_____

_____

_____

21. Draw a picture of your family.

Student Name: _____ Date: _____

Journal Entry

Because this chapter attempted to put you into close contact with a set of significant day-to-day responsibilities of classroom teachers, your Journal Entry should concentrate on what you have learned about these important areas of classroom teaching. Specifically, focus on what you have learned about one or more of the following:

1. Lesson planning and lesson implementation in general.
2. Lesson planning and implementation in specific grade levels.
3. Classroom management.
4. Classroom questioning.
5. Student–teacher interaction and dialogue.
6. Technology in the learning environment.
7. Cooperative learning.

Questions for Discussion

1. You have had the opportunity to observe many different lessons as a result of chapter activities. As you consider these lessons, what characteristic of the lessons was memorable, intriguing, or surprising to you, and why was this the case?

2. Following through on selected activities in this chapter, you may have had the opportunity to observe teachers with varying levels of experience. What struck you as noteworthy about the comparative as well as individual performance of these teachers?

3. Most education researchers describe the American classroom as a complex place.
   a. Did your observations of classroom interaction leave you with this impression?
   b. If so, as a prospective teacher, how did you feel about this complexity?
   c. If not, what feelings were associated with your observations of classroom interaction?

4. The interaction between one teacher and twenty-five to thirty-five students in the context of a lesson is a special type of patterned interaction and communication, but it is not unlike the patterned interaction that occurs in several other organizational settings. What did the classroom interaction that you observed remind you of, if anything? In what ways was the classroom interaction similar to interaction that you have observed or experienced in another setting? Does this similarity have any implications for your future career as a teacher? If so, please identify and discuss.

References

American Association of University Women. (1992). *How schools shortchange girls: The AAUW report.* West Haven, CT: NEA Professional Library. A summary of the report is available from the AAUW sales office (800-225-9998).

Brophy, J. E. (1983). Research on the self-fulfilling prophecy and teacher expectations. *Journal of Educational Psychology, 75(5),* 631–666.

Campbell, P. B. (1986). What's a nice girl like you doing in a math class? *Phi Delta Kappan, 67(7),* 516–519.

Davidman, L., and Davidman, P. (2001). *Teaching with a multicultural perspective: A practical guide* (3rd ed.). White Plains, NY: Longman.

Educational Testing Service. (1995). *Teacher performance assessments: Assessment criteria.* Princeton, New Jersey.

Good, T. L. (1987). Two decades of research on teacher expectations: Findings and future directions. *Journal of Teacher Education, 38(4),* 32–47.

Good, T. L., and Brophy, J. E. (2003). *Looking in classrooms* (9th ed.). Boston, MA: Allyn & Bacon.

Marzano, R. J., Pickering, O. J., and Pollock, J. E. (2001). *Classroom instruction that works: Research-based strategies for increasing student achievement.* Alexandria, VA: Association for Supervision and Curriculum Development.

Rist, R. C. (1987). Do teachers count in the lives of children? *Educational Researcher, 16(19),* 41–42.

Rowe, M. B. (1974). Wait time and rewards as instructional variables, their influences on language, logic, and fate control. *Journal of Research in Science Teaching, 11(2),* 81–94.

Sadker, M., and Sadker, D. (1986). Sexism in the classroom: From grade school to graduate school. *Phi Delta Kappan, 67(7),* 512–515.

Slavin, R. E. (1995). *Cooperative learning: Theory, research, and practice* (2nd ed.). Boston, MA: Allyn & Bacon.

Tobin, K. (1986, Summer). Effects of teacher wait time on discourse characteristics in math and language arts classrooms. *American Educational Research Journal, 23(2),* 191–200.

Tobin, K. (1987). The role of wait time in higher cognitive level learning. *Review of Educational Research, 57(1),* 69–95.

Varlas, L. (2005). Bridging the widest gap: Raising the achievement of black boys. *Education Update, 47(8),* 1–3, 8.

Wineburg, S. S. (1987). The self-fulfillment of the self-fulfilling prophecy. *Educational Researcher, 16(9),* 28–37.

Chapter 5

DEVELOPING INTERVIEWING SKILLS

This chapter is one of several in this text in which you will utilize interviewing. Although the focus will be on classroom teachers as a source of information, you will also have the opportunity to practice interviewing with classmates, student teachers, and college professors. Before placing you into the interview setting, we will give you specific information on how and whom to interview in P–12 settings.

All the interview tasks in this text are valuable because they have you, a prospective teacher, use an exciting learning strategy to conduct teaching-related research right at the beginning of your career. These interview tasks require you to be outgoing, articulate, well organized, patient, and a good listener; and the time you put into them will be well invested. You will see your interviews expand and modify the interpretations that you placed on various observed events. Many of you will be assigned to a teacher or will spend more time with a particular teacher during your early field experience; and through the interview process you may experience your first face-to-face professional exchange with a P–12 practitioner. With these interviews, you will begin your initiation into the rich dialogue about teaching that is occurring in many P–12 programs in this era of educational change.

In this chapter we focus on the structured interview and its derivative, the semistructured interview. We choose this focus even though we know you will derive much useful information from the informal, spontaneous discussions that you will have with teachers in a variety of settings. Although informal interviews definitely have their time and place, the semistructured interview is a particularly appropriate tool for prospective teachers who are trying to make contact with professional educators in the busy world that teachers inhabit. This will be even more true for the outstanding teachers whom we encourage you to seek out; in most cases their reputations are due to the extra time and energy they put into their classrooms. This type of teacher may find it difficult to make time for a meandering, unfocused interview. You will also discover that the planned interview will work for you—first in helping to get you the interview and then in helping you to derive the maximum amount of useful information in what will usually be a short time, perhaps twenty to thirty minutes. Let us now take a closer look at structured and semistructured interviews.

THE STRUCTURED INTERVIEW

The structured interview has several distinctive characteristics. In a structured interview the questions are written in advance, and the phrasing and content of the questions are checked to ensure that the questions are clear and easy to interpret. In addition, you will arrange the questions in a sequential, logical manner; try to match the number of questions to the amount of time planned for the interview; and write a statement explaining the purpose of the interview. After you have selected the questions, tried them out on friends, and put them into final form, you'll lay out the questions on a notepad, with a page allocated for each question, to facilitate note taking during the interview.

After these steps, you will be ready to call the teacher to arrange a time and place for the interview. The first contact will likely be with a school secretary, and you should be organized, polite, and appreciative as the secretary tries to find out when the teacher will have a break during the day. After making contact with the teacher, you should tell the teacher

1. Your name and position within a specific teacher education program (a sophomore at Bowling Green State University, a postbaccalaureate candidate about to enter the teacher education program, or the like).
2. That you would like to arrange a twenty- or thirty-minute interview.
3. The kinds of questions you intend to ask (two or three examples of your questions) and the purpose of the interview.
4. The kind of flexibility that you have for the interview ("I can show up at your school between noon and 2:00 P.M. on a Monday, Wednesday, or Friday").

Before we discuss the actual questions that make up a structured interview, we should mention that during an interview it is natural and appropriate for the structured interview to drift into a semistructured one. This transformation occurs if you, the interviewer, choose to build on the answer to one question by asking a new, unplanned question. This is analogous to the situation that occurs every day in classrooms when teachers diverge from their lesson plans to exploit that uniquely fertile circumstance commonly called the "teachable moment." In the context of interviews carried out by novice interviewers, an apt label for a transition to a semistructured interview would be the "questionable moment." Such divergence is both practical and highly recommended. The amount of time spent on the interview will likely be the same. Some planned questions may not get asked, but they can be included in your next interview. You will find that your interview will be more enjoyable and probably more revealing when you add questions to your structured interview, particularly if you follow the interview guidelines described later in the chapter.

THE INTERVIEW QUESTIONS

You might well be wondering what comes first: the teacher or the interview? We recommend that you develop your interview first and then use your questions and interview rationale to help land your interview. However, it would be practical to think about the kind of teacher you want to interview as you develop your questions. For example, you might decide that your first interview will be with a kindergarten teacher, a junior high school science teacher, or a high school English, speech, or history teacher. Focusing on a particular category of teacher will make it easier to generate questions specific to grade level and course content. For example, here are some questions appropriate for tenth-grade biology teachers:

1. What kinds of laboratory experiences are a common part of the curriculum at this high school?
2. To what extent is the high school biology curriculum career-oriented?

After focusing on a particular type of teacher, the next logical step in the interview development process is to brainstorm and generate a randomly ordered set of questions. After the questions exist, the sequencing and refining process can begin. At this point you may be wondering, Do I generate these questions all by myself? Typically the answer is no. There are at least five sources of questions, which in combination will produce an abundant crop of appropriate questions. These sources are the classrooms in which you observe, the professors in your teacher education program, your own curiosity, sample questions included in this text (see, for example, Table 5.1), and finally, questions shared by your fellow students.

To illustrate more clearly how a structured interview is developed, let's walk through the development process step-by-step. As we proceed, you will draw on a set of general questions for structured interviews (see Table 5.1). This set of questions includes personal background questions that we suggest you use at the beginning of all, or most, teacher interviews.

THE STRUCTURED INTERVIEW DEVELOPMENT PROCESS

I. First pick a category of teacher. For example, our category will be a sixth-grade teacher.

II. Next generate a list of questions.
   A. Select questions from Table 5.1. For our example we will select the following questions from Table 5.1: 1, 2, 4, 7, 9, 10, 11, 12, 14, and 15.
   B. Add other questions that stem from your observations in upper-grade elementary school classrooms, your own curiosity, and suggestions from your professors and fellow students. Questions such as the ones that follow will probably result:
      1. Why is it, in several classes I have observed, that reading is taught in small groups and math in large groups?
      2. Why do you have the children seated in little clusters of four desks facing each other?
      3. Is the sixth grade a unique or special grade to teach? If so, what makes it special? In what ways is it different than the fourth or fifth grade?
      4. Do you have textbooks to help teach most of the separate elementary school content areas?
      5. Does the school perceive some content areas to be more important than others? How does this attitude influence the structure and actual delivery of the school curriculum?
      6. How does teaching in the upper elementary grades differ from teaching in the lower grades?
      7. When did you discover that you were going to be an upper elementary teacher?

TABLE 5.1
General Questions for Structured Interviews

1. Before I ask you more specific questions about the teaching profession, could you tell me a bit about your background as a teacher?
   a. Years of experience?
   b. Grade levels taught?
   c. Numbers of years teaching at this school? In this school district?
2. What have you found most satisfying in your career in teaching?
3. What has been the most unsatisfying element in your teaching career?
4. In the positive sense of the word, do you consider teaching to be a challenging profession? If so, what challenges have made teaching an interesting career for you?
5. Do you consider teaching to be a profession? Why? Why not?
6. What do you do to keep yourself rejuvenated or enthusiastic about teaching?
7. Do you belong to a teachers' organization? If so, which one(s)?
   a. How do these organizations help teachers?
   b. Is there a negative side to teachers' organizations?
8. If you were starting out all over and just about to begin a teacher education program, on which teaching skills or areas of knowledge would you place extra effort?
9. What important changes have occurred in the profession of teaching during your teaching career?
10. How do you think the role of teacher may change in the next five to ten years?
11. During your career in teaching, has teaching become a more interesting job? A more difficult job? What has made it more interesting and/or more difficult?
12. What is the job like after school is out? Do you find yourself bringing home schoolwork after school or on weekends? On the average, how many hours per week do you put into your teaching?
13. Are computers and videotapes widely used in your school? In your classroom? If so, for what purpose?
14. Are there specific books, courses, or workshop experiences that have been particularly meaningful to you as a teacher? If so, could you briefly describe them?
15. What or who helped you decide to become a teacher, and what or who helped you choose to remain a teacher?
16. How did you end up teaching at your current grade level? If you had the opportunity to start all over again, would you obtain a credential to teach at another level—say, high school instead of elementary school?
17. What do you do that is particularly effective with students?
18. Would you recommend teaching as a career for your own children? Why? Why not?
19. What advice would you give to someone like me who is at an early stage of the teacher education process?

In what ways are interviewing skills essential to effective communication between teachers and parents, students, and other teachers?

"Well, you see, Mrs. Smith, the reason your son is doing poorly in school is that he's dumb."

Used with permission of the cartoonist—Tom McCally
Holt, Rinehart and Winston

III. Now comes the sequencing and refining step. We will arbitrarily select a fifteen-question limit for this structured interview. This means that we could select five of the questions just listed, integrate them with the ten questions from Table 5.1, and then work out a logical sequence. Here are fifteen questions listed in random order. Rearrange them to create your own logical sequence and then compare it with the sequential structured interview schedule that we have created. Discuss any differences with fellow students and/or your instructor.

The Random List

1. Why is it that reading is taught in small groups in your class and math in large groups (based on prior observation in the teacher's class)?

2. What or who helped you decide to become a teacher, and what or who helped you choose to remain a teacher?

3. How do you think the role of teacher may change in the next ten years?

4. Do you consider teaching to be a challenging profession, in the positive sense of the word? If so, what challenges have made teaching an interesting career for you?

5. How does teaching in the sixth grade differ from teaching in the first grade?

6. What have you found most satisfying in your career in teaching?

7. What is the job like after school is out? Do you find yourself bringing home schoolwork after school or on weekends?

8. Do school administrators think that some content areas are more important than others? How do these beliefs influence the actual content and delivery of the school curriculum?

9. Before I ask you more specific questions about the teaching profession, could you tell me a bit about your background in teaching?
   a. Years of experience?
   b. Grade levels taught?
   c. Numbers of years teaching at this school? In this school district?

10. Do you belong to a teachers' organization? If so, which one(s)?
    a. How do these organizations help teachers?
    b. Do they create any problems for the profession?

11. When did you discover that you were going to be an upper elementary teacher?

12. What important changes in the teaching profession have occurred during your teaching career?

13. Do you have textbooks to help you teach most of the separate elementary school content areas?

14. During your career in teaching, has teaching become a more interesting job? A more difficult job? What has made it more interesting or more difficult?

15. What advice would you give to a student considering a career in teaching in today's world?

The Sequenced Structured Interview Schedule

1. Before I ask you more specific questions about the teaching profession, could you tell me a bit about your background in teaching?
   a. Years of experience?
   b. Grade levels taught?
   c. Number of years teaching at this school? In this school district?

2. What have you found most satisfying in your career in teaching?

3. Do you consider teaching to be a challenging profession, in the positive sense of the word? If so, what challenges have made teaching an interesting career for you?

4. What important changes in the teaching profession have occurred during your teaching career?

5. How do you think the role of teacher may change in the next five to ten years?

6. During your career in teaching, has teaching become a more interesting job? A more difficult job? What has made it more interesting and/or more difficult?

7. What is the job like after school is out? Do you find yourself bringing home schoolwork after school or on weekends?

8. Do you belong to a teachers' organization? If so, which one(s)?
   a. How do these organizations help teachers?
   b. Do they create any problems for the profession?

9. What or who helped you decide to become a teacher, and what or who helped you choose to remain a teacher?

10. How does teaching in the sixth grade differ from teaching in the first grade?

11. When did you discover that you were going to be an upper elementary teacher?

12. Do you have textbooks to help you teach all of the separate elementary school content areas?

13. Do school administrators think that some content areas are more important than others? How do these beliefs influence the actual content and delivery of the school curriculum?

14. Why is reading taught in small groups in your class and math in large groups (based on prior observation in the teacher's class)?

15. What advice would you give to a student considering a career in teaching in today's world?

Now that you have sequenced questions, you are ready to write the purpose of your interview: your *interview rationale*. When you first talk to the teacher, you will use this short statement to help win your interview with a busy educator. Following is an example of an interview rationale for the listed sequence of questions. Please note that your statement should be direct and to the point.

INTERVIEW RATIONALE EXAMPLE

"My purpose in seeking this interview is to learn more about the teaching profession from people in the profession. I want to learn as much as I can about teaching as a possible career for myself."

Interview Guidelines

As in most complex endeavors, there are a few rules or guidelines in interviewing that, if followed, will help you have a positive experience. We will list some *do*s and *don't*s for interviewing. Here are the *do*s:

1. Be aware as you go out for your interviews that you represent your teacher education program as well as yourself.

2. Realize that both you and your teacher education program are striving to develop and maintain a positive reputation with the teachers in your region. Therefore, try to represent yourself and your program well.

3. Treat the data you collect as semiconfidential information. You will share observations related to your data with your professors and fellow students, but you need not and should not use the teacher's name in these discussions. There is no instructional advantage in using names, but there is the clear possibility that some misunderstanding may develop if teachers come to believe that they are being unprofessionally, and unethically, evaluated.

4. Be exceedingly polite and patient as you interact with your interviewee and other school personnel.

5. Dress professionally for your interview; in your particular region, find out what that means.

6. Be early, and arrive well organized and prepared to take notes.

7. On the day before the interview, call the school to leave a polite reminder about the interview. You can ask a school secretary to place a brief note in the teacher's

mailbox: "Dear Mr./Ms. Smith, I am looking forward to our interview tomorrow and will meet you at your room as planned."

8. Conduct your interview in a private setting such as the teacher's classroom or the school library.

9. Follow up the interview with a brief thank-you note. Write this note the day after the interview, and either mail it to the teacher at the school, or drop it off at the school to be placed in the teacher's mailbox. The more promptly you write this note, the easier it will be for you to make the note personal and relevant to the interview, and the more the teacher will appreciate receiving it.

Here are the *don'ts*:

1. Don't bring a tape recorder or even ask to use a tape recorder on your first visit; our experience suggests that the pressure of the tape recorder, during the first meeting, makes the interview excessively formal.

2. Don't interrupt your interviewee to comment on his or her responses; remember that you are there to hear his or her replies to your questions.

3. Don't interview your teacher in the teachers' lounge or any other public space in the school. (You'll risk too many interruptions.)

4. Don't ask questions that could be perceived as rude, pushy, or offensive. Examples of such questions include the following:
   a. "Do you get along with the principal of your school?" Or worse: "Do you like the principal of your school?"
   b. "How much money does a teacher with your experience make?" (You can find this out at the school district office by asking for the district salary schedule.)
   c. "Why does this school have such a drab environment?"
   d. "Doesn't the low status of the teaching profession bother you?"
   e. "All I see are older teachers in this school. Don't they hire young teachers in this district?"
   f. "The kids in this school really look messy. Does that affect their schoolwork?"

Please note that Questions 4a–4f ask about things that are natural for you to be curious about. But on your first or second visit these questions would be unnatural and inappropriate for a relative stranger to ask. We mention the second visit because we have learned that structured interviews can easily lead to a follow-up observation and a second interview. When the interview has gone well, the interviewer can say to the teacher, "You know, Mrs. Sanchez, I really enjoyed today's interview and learned quite a bit; do you think I could possibly spend some time observing in your class?" A semistructured interview would likely follow the observation.

At this point you should be feeling more confident about carrying out a structured interview with a teacher. You have a clear idea about what a structured interview is, how to develop one, and how to use an interview rationale to set up your interview. You have also learned about the concern that a teacher education program might have about its image and about your responsibilities to that program and to your own future. We now discuss several other important interview-related questions:

1. How do you decide exactly whom to call for an interview?

2. After the interview has been arranged, how do you organize yourself for data collection and data analysis?

3. What do you do with the set of interview data that results from your interviews?

Whom Do You Interview?

This fundamentally important question might lead you to ask, "Why not go out and interview any teacher who is willing to be interviewed?" Indeed, there would be some wisdom in doing this. But there is too much variety in our profession to opt for this strategy. Our experience suggests that the teachers who can best help you decide whether teaching is the right career for you are teachers who have experienced success in their own careers. Thus we recommend that you contact the teachers who have been selected by the professors in your teacher education program or ones recommended by these selected teachers.

Collecting and Organizing Your Data

To collect data during and after your interview, we recommend that you employ the "key word–scribble–download" strategy. This strategy involves these steps:

1. Type or write your questions into an interview schedule, leaving three or four inches of space between the questions (the interview schedule is your sequenced, refined list of questions). Then make a photocopy of your schedule. Thus you enter your interview with two copies of your interview schedule.

2. Using your first copy of the interview schedule, scribble key words or phrases from the teacher's responses to each question while maintaining ongoing eye contact with the teacher (a neat trick and something that you'll get better at).

3. Using your key words and phrases and your second copy of the interview schedule, write down your thoughts immediately after (within an hour of) the interview. During this "download" phase you will use your key words and memory to write a more complete, extended description of the teacher's reply to each question. These extended descriptions provide the data for the analysis and synthesis described later.

4. Read what you have just written in Step 3, and on the same or a separate sheet list any new questions that stem from data in your notes.

Data Analysis and Synthesis

Data analysis is something you should do for each individual interview as well as when the notes from several interviews have accumulated.

To begin, a day or two after each individual interview, you should examine your extended notes to see if you have anything to add to them. Occasionally you will remember something two days after the interview that was overlooked during downloading, and sometimes you will see something in your notes that leads to a new awareness of what the teacher meant by a certain remark. The examination might also suggest new questions for a second interview with the same teacher, or the questions might be used with a revised interview schedule for a new teacher.

Later, when you have extended notes from several interviews, a different type of analysis will be appropriate. At that point you will be in a position to compare, contrast, and make inferences based on the data you have collected. After you have reread all your interview notes and studied the points of similarity and contrast, it would be fruitful to answer the following question in your mind *and* on paper:

From these interviews and (perhaps) follow-up observations, what have I (tentatively) learned or decided about teaching and the teaching profession?

Your written response to this question will be your data synthesis, and it will help you extract from the interview data the knowledge that will inform and influence your later observations, interviews, and decisions about a career in teaching. Some of these thoughts could be explored in greater depth in your journal notes.

ACTIVITIES FOR CHAPTER 5

Because this chapter focuses on the design and implementation of semistructured interviews, all of the activities here will involve you in this type of interview. The activities that we have selected, and their organization, assume two things. First, some of you will be assigned to one main cooperating teacher during your early field experience. Second, the interview with your assigned teacher will be most fruitful if carried out in the middle of the quarter or semester. At the same time, we encourage you to design and carry out brief semistructured interviews as soon as possible; your classmates, professors, student teachers in your program, and spouse or significant other can help you sharpen your interviewing skills and perhaps brighten your day (provided that you ask them the right questions).

Core Activity
THE SEMISTRUCTURED INTERVIEW

Design and conduct a semistructured interview with your cooperating teacher or a veteran teacher (who has eight to twenty-five years of experience). Use the key word–scribble–download strategy to develop a database from each interview. When the database is established, analyze your data to answer this question:

> From the actual interview, and from my analysis of the data generated by the interview, what have I learned about teaching and/or the teaching profession?

Suggested Activity 1

THE NEW TEACHER

Repeat the Core Activity; however, this time interview teachers who have been teaching for two to five years. After responding to the "What have I learned about teaching and/or the teaching profession?" question, compare and contrast the responses of the veteran and new teachers.

Suggested Activity 2

THE AWARD-WINNING TEACHER

Design and conduct a semistructured interview with an award-winning teacher, possibly the county or school district teacher of the year. This interview should be conducted by two members of your class in front of the whole class and could be videotaped by the instructor for later use.

Suggested Activity 3

THE COLLEGE INSTRUCTOR

Design and conduct a semistructured interview with your favorite college instructor. During your interview (and observation) of this instructor, try to identify and then describe the elements of this instructor's teaching style that seem most significant to you. If you choose this activity, the following questions may prove helpful:

1. What characteristics or behaviors combine to make this instructor so successful?
2. What characteristics make this instructor a special, almost unique teacher?
3. Which aspects of this instructor's teaching style or behavioral performance appear to be artistic?

Suggested Activity 4
THE TYPICAL TEACHER'S DAY

Now that you've had the opportunity to orient yourself physically within the school building and the classroom, you will find it helpful to orient yourself to a typical day in the life of a teacher. Although most teachers would say that none of their days are typical, careful observation and some well-stated questions should give you a reasonably clear picture of how your cooperating teacher spends his or her time.

The core of the teacher's daily activities will be the courses or content areas that he or she teaches. Using those as the cornerstones of your teacher's daily time grid, complete the grid that follows by questioning the teacher about the following:

1. What time does the teacher usually arrive at school?

_____

_____

2. What kinds of activities does the teacher engage in between arriving at school and the beginning of classes? Any special duties or regularly scheduled meetings?

_____

_____

_____

_____

3. How is the teacher's time spent between classes and/or during free periods, lunch, recess, and so on?

_____

_____

_____

_____

4. During class time, is the teacher constantly directing instruction, or are free times* built into the teaching schedule?

_____

---

*Free times could be segments of time when students do seatwork and the teacher grades papers or handles routine administrative paperwork.

_____

_____

_____

5. Ask the teacher to estimate the percentage of his or her daily time that is spent in noninstructional activities (e.g., bus duty, lunchroom duty, administrative paperwork, calling parents, collecting money, checking attendance).

_____

_____

6. How much time does the teacher spend in the building after school? Is that by choice? What activities usually take up after-school time?

_____

_____

_____

_____

7. What extracurricular activities is the teacher in charge of? How much time do they take per day?

_____

_____

_____

_____

8. Ask the teacher to estimate the total number of hours that he or she spends per day in school-related activities.

_____

_____

THE TEACHER'S DAY

On the grid that follows, indicate the predominant activities during the teacher's waking hours. In the space provided, indicate the duration of the activity and whether it was school-related or nonschool-related time.

Time	Description of Activity	School Related	Nonschool Related
5:00 A.M. to 6:00 A.M.			
to 7:00 A.M.			
to 8:00 A.M.			
to 9:00 A.M.			
to 10:00 A.M.			
to 11:00 A.M.			
to noon			
to 1:00 P.M.			
to 2:00 P.M.			
to 3:00 P.M.			
to 4:00 P.M.			
to 5:00 P.M.			
to 6:00 P.M.			
to 7:00 P.M.			

to 8:00 P.M.	
to 9:00 P.M.	
to 10:00 P.M.	
to 11:00 P.M.	
to midnight	

TABULATE THE FOLLOWING:

1. Total number of hours in teacher's typical workday: _____

2. Percentage of time spent in school-related activities: _____%

3. Percentage of time spent in nonschool-related activities: _____%

4. Percentage of school-related activities that are noninstructional: _____%

5. Total number of hours spent teaching or performing instructionally related activities (setting up labs, learning centers, etc.): _____

Although the public's general impression is that teachers work from 8:30 A.M. to 3:30 P.M. and have June, July, and August for vacation time, nothing could be further from the truth. Teachers' days are usually long, and their schedules rarely allow much time for relaxation. During the day, free time consists mainly of stolen moments because even unscheduled periods are consumed with preparing for class, grading papers, or calling parents. In addition, the three months' summer vacation is often spent taking additional graduate coursework, supplementing the yearly income, or in some cases both.

To fully appreciate the rigors of teaching, we must analyze the amount of time spent doing school-related activities and the physical and emotional effects of the intensive nature of the work. Introducing yourself to schools and teaching requires a thorough assessment of the environments in which teaching occurs and of the conditions under which teachers perform their daily teaching and nonteaching routines. Even a cursory analysis provides convincing evidence that a considerable gap exists between the public's general impressions and the realities of the teaching profession.

Student Name: _____   Date: _____

Journal Entry

Because this chapter focused on interviewing classroom teachers, your Journal Entry should comment or elaborate on the following:

1. What have you learned from the set of interviews that you conducted?

2. What are your thoughts about interviewing as a research strategy? Was it a strategy that worked for you, or did you find it difficult to gather information in the face-to-face mode? What did you like about the interviewing process? What, if anything, would you do differently in your next interview?

_____

_____

_____

_____

_____

_____

_____

_____

_____

_____

_____

_____

_____

_____

_____

_____

_____

_____

_____

_____

_____

_____

_____

_____

_____

_____

_____

_____

_____

_____

_____

_____

_____

_____

Questions for Discussion

1. For a variety of reasons, in the past as well as in the present, the teaching profession has had an extremely high turnover rate. When you consider your future in teaching, do you perceive yourself as someone who will become a veteran teacher?

2. In the next chapter, "Images of the Teacher," we note that the public has not always viewed teaching and the teaching profession in a positive light. Given the data derived from the interviews in this chapter and the observations and interviews conducted in previous chapters, what is your view of the teaching profession? More specifically,

   a. Do you consider teaching to be a profession? Why or why not?

   b. Do you believe that teaching is a profession or career that you will find satisfying and in which you will be able to take pride? Why or why not?

3. The teachers you interviewed had the opportunity to discuss changes that might occur in the role of teacher in the next ten years. Comment on the responses made by the teachers, and then ask the instructor of your course the same question.

4. Where and how do you think interviewing might fit into your approach to teaching?

References

Chang, V. N., and Scott, S. T. (1999). *Basic interviewing skills: A workbook for practitioners*. Belmont, CA: Wadsworth.

Edenborough, R. (2002). *Effective interviewing: A handbook of skills and techniques* (2nd ed.). Boulder, CO: Netlibrary.

Grobel, L. (2004). *The art of the interview: Lessons from a master of the craft*. New York: Three Rivers Press.

Holstem, J., and Gubrium, J. F. (Eds.). (2003). *Inside interviewing: New lenses, new concerns*. Thousand Oaks, CA: Sage Publications.

Kyale, S. (1996). *Interviews: An introduction to qualitative research interviewing*. Thousand Oaks, CA: Sage Publications.

Metzler, K. (1996). *Creative interviewing: The writer's guide to gathering information by asking questions* (3rd ed.). Boston: Allyn and Bacon.

Perlich, M. (2001). *The art of the interview: A step by step guide to insightful interviewing*. Philadelphia: Xlibris.

Rubin, H. J., and Rubin, I. (2005). *Qualitative interviewing: The art of hearing data* (2nd ed.). Thousand Oaks, CA: Sage Publications.

Chapter 6

IMAGES OF THE TEACHER

Up to this point you've been directing your observations and your thinking toward the school and the people who work in it. You've begun the process of examining what occurs in school buildings and classrooms and why some schools seem more successful than others in reaching their goals. Because your primary purpose is to discover whether you want to become a teacher, however, the role or image of the teacher in the school is of critical importance. The focus of this chapter is on the teacher, or rather on the image of the teacher, and how that image has affected your perception of the teaching profession. You may be surprised to discover that the image of teachers that you've come to accept is a function of both your own experience in schools and the depiction of teachers by others who influence you in conscious and unconscious ways.

Because of these influences, your decision to enter teaching will be shaped by this combination of experiences in school and images of teachers presented in books, newspapers, movies, and television. Teachers, like doctors and lawyers, are often inviting targets for media stereotypes. However, doctors and lawyers, unlike teachers, are often presented as dedicated professionals employing considerable intelligence and occasional wit in solving the perplexing problems of their professions with the latest practices and technologies. Conversely, teachers are rarely shown as doing more than handling "problem" students or unsympathetic administrators.* Although television viewers are frequently given insights into the courtroom practices of talented lawyers and the operating room techniques of skilled surgeons, teachers are usually shown employing the most traditional methodologies (lectures and discussions) with students who are generally eager for periods of somewhere around five minutes. Not surprisingly, teaching usually looks easy under those conditions. Only recently have the media begun to portray teachers in realistic, more positive roles.

What of these images? To what extent do they influence our perceptions of teachers and teaching? How accurate are they? What impact have they had on teachers currently in the profession? The answers to some of these questions, of course, will be found during your observations and interviews with teachers. Others, however, lie

---

*Interestingly, principals are almost always presented unsympathetically as autocratic pencil pushers thoroughly wrapped up in maintaining the bureaucracy at all costs. In that sense, they usually come off as looking worse than the teachers.

within you because you have had your perceptions molded and "massaged" by the media. In the next section we'll explore how some of these images have been created by various media and then gauge how much these images have influenced you. Then you'll pose some of these same questions to classroom teachers to determine how much they see of themselves and others in these images.

THE TEACHER IN LITERATURE, FILM, AND TELEVISION

From Washington Irving's characterization of Ichabod Crane as a hapless pedagogue immersed in his own self-importance and fears, to Mark Twain's depiction of the one-room schoolmaster who sneaks a peek at *Gray's Anatomy* and has his "dome gilded" (his bald head painted gold) by Tom Sawyer and his friends, to the more sympathetic, two-dimensional view of the young, but obviously misguided, progressive elementary teacher in Harper Lee's *To Kill a Mockingbird*, the treatment of teachers in literature has only occasionally been positive.

Female teachers in literature are often depicted as unattractive physically, undesirable sexually, and unskilled socially, as opposed to the well-dressed, physically attractive female lawyers seen on *Law and Order* and *Boston Legal*. The "schoolmarm" image remains the dominant perspective of many writers. Male teachers fare little better, although they are occasionally shown as having lustful yearnings for a two-dimensional female character. These yearnings, however, inevitably lead to the teacher's downfall in the community. The literary message is clear. Teachers are ordinary-looking, asexual, moderately intelligent (though often in an eccentric way), socially inept public servants. Their ambitions are minimal and limited primarily to salvaging some recalcitrant student(s). Females are teaching only until they can find a suitable mate or, because of a jilted love, until they become schoolmarmish spinsters. More recently, however, novels by Judy Blume and others have presented teachers in a realistic, positive light, and these literary images may have affected your perceptions of teaching.

Research on Hollywood films over the past fifty years suggests that teachers have fared as poorly in that medium as they have in literature. Teachers in films made before the 1970s are frequently shown as pedantic, dull, and sometimes cruel to their students. Even when teachers are depicted as sympathetic to the needs of adolescents, they are also shown as being confused by the actions of young people and dismayed by the differences in the basic values held by the students and themselves. It appears in numerous cases that the teachers have had little formal training in psychology, pedagogy, and philosophy and have literally stepped in front of the class with little more than the force of their personalities to see them through.

Even when teachers are depicted in a generally positive light in books and films such as Sidney Poitier in *To Sir with Love*, Nick Nolte in *Teachers*, William Hurt in *Children of a Lesser God*, Robin Williams in *Dead Poets Society*, Michelle Pfeiffer in *Dangerous Minds*, and Richard Dreyfuss in *Mr. Holland's Opus*, they are shown as struggling against enormous odds and at great personal cost. Frequently, despite their best efforts, these teachers are defeated by "the system." Teachers, it appears, must be social misfits, crusading missionaries, or superheroes. These images can create an unrealistic view of education and teaching, particularly when contrasted to the realities of classroom life in most schools. Rarely does one find a Mr. Chips or a Mr. Holland or a Miss Jean Brodie in elementary or secondary classrooms and schools. When portrayed as larger than life in film, characters like Mr. Holland have a way of blending with our actual experiences in schools to create a curious mixture of fantasy and reality in our unconscious. Indeed, even the inspiring teachers such as Michelle Pfeiffer in *Dangerous Minds*, Robin Williams in *Dead Poet's Society*, and Richard Dreyfuss in *Mr. Holland's Opus* leave the profession due to frustration over the insurmountable odds (*Dangerous Minds*) or are forced out of their positions by an unsympathetic administration that can't handle students who think critically and rebel (*Dead Poet's Society*). Mr. Holland was forced into early retirement because of supposed budget cuts that eliminated "frills" such as music education. Certainly this creates the image that good and inspiring teachers are expendable or simply give up.

In the past few years, teachers and schools have begun to play less of a role in films. Schools have tended to become settings for action, but the action is not inherent in the school itself. Teachers tend to be depicted as characters in the setting rather than as figures designed to present teachers in an inspirational light. Such vehicles as *The School of Rock*, *The Substitute*, and *Harry Potter* use schools as locations in which the action will occur rather than providing any real insights into the teaching profession or the act of teaching as desirable. Because of the prolonged and frequently intense nature of our school experiences, as opposed to our limited experience with doctors and lawyers, film images can have a powerful effect on our recollection of teachers in a manner that is unlike our recollection of any other profession.

Television images have an impact on perceptions that frequently exceeds that of film. Films depict memorable people, whereas television depicts memorable characters. The image of the teacher, as depicted by television writers, has evolved in a curious manner over the past five decades. In the 1950s teachers were seen as comedic individuals who had to maintain their resolute calmness when faced with the light-hearted antics of their students (e.g., *Our Miss Brooks*). In the 1960s and early 1970s the serious-minded, student-centered teachers such as Mr. Novak or Pete Dixon (*Room 222*) appeared on the school scene to guide their frequently troubled charges through adolescence. Although sometimes humorous, these teachers were never comedic. No doubt many of your teachers in school were influenced by some of these images as they made their decision to enter teaching. Indeed, during this period (1965–1975) more people entered teaching than during any other decade before or since.

The late 1970s ushered in the teacher as stand-up comedian when the Sweathogs welcomed back Kotter (Gabe Kaplan).* Here the teacher was totally immersed in the lives of his students, and they in his. This, of course, was because he had been "one of them," proving that in teaching, unlike in any other profession, you *can* go home again. Although essentially a situation comedy and vehicle for Gabe Kaplan, this popular series portrayed the teacher as caring, clever, and, on the whole, serious and positive. Kotter's positive teacher image is in the same vein as the images of the hardworking, intelligent teachers of *Room 222* and the generally positive images presented in the New York City–based television series *Fame*. In the 1980s comedy

*According to the *Houston Chronicle*, Gabe Kaplan's character on *Welcome Back, Kotter* has been named the Most Memorable Teacher on Television by *Inside TV* magazine. The magazine recognizes Gabe Kotter, the high school teacher from the 1970s sitcom that also starred John Travolta. Also on the list: cartoon character Edna Krabappel of *The Simpsons*, Lydia Grant (Debbie Allen) of *Fame*, Charlie Moore (Howard Hesseman) of *Head of the Class*, Laura Ingalls (Melissa Gilbert) of *Little House on the Prairie*, Ross Geller (David Schwimmer) of *Friends*, Mark Cooper (Mark Curry) of *Hangin' with Mr. Cooper*, Fonzie (Henry Winkler) of *Happy Days*, Carol Vessey (Julie Bowen) of *Ed*, and Max Medina (Scott Cohen) of *Gilmore Girls*.

and dramatic series continued this more positive portrayal of teachers and, to some extent, administrators. In *Head of the Class* a nomadic substitute teacher was drawn into a class of gifted students. He was shown as student-centered, comic-serious, and thoroughly dedicated to his gifted "Sweathogs."

In the late 1990s to the present the image of the teacher on television began to shift somewhat. Although medical shows such as *E.R.* and *Chicago Hope* show innovative medical techniques and the sometimes routine, sometimes hectic life of an emergency room, schools and classrooms still tend to be drawn from the same visual images that dominated in the 1950s. By the late 1990s *The Practice* and its more recent incarnation, *Boston Legal*, and *Law and Order* showed how exciting and stimulating the legal profession could be, whereas recent police dramas such as *N.Y.P.D. Blue, Law and Order: Special Victims Unit*, and *Law and Order: Criminal Intent* showed the gritty side of being a detective in a major city. The profession of forensic science has also been given significant prominence through the three series *CSI, CSI: Miami*, and *CSI: New York*, all of which provide a detailed (and sometimes unrealistic) view of the nexus of modern technology and old-fashioned detective work. Interestingly, this has proven to be a major boon to science teachers trying to convince students that science really is interesting and exciting! Whether in an emergency room, a courtroom, a squad room, or a forensics lab, doctors, lawyers, police officers, and crime scene investigators are shown as having interesting and challenging *professions*.

Unfortunately, the same can't be said for classroom teachers. Neither their jobs nor the places where they work (classrooms) are shown with any depth of understanding. If teachers have interesting, exciting, or challenging lives, it is because of the *people* with whom they interact (students, parents, community members), not the *profession*. As one critic noted, in the 1960s and 1970s television shows about school showed that "the teachers really wanted to teach, the students weren't smarter than the teacher, and you actually learned a thing or two you could find in a book." By 2005, however, the teaching profession and life in schools were only a peripheral part of television viewing. Teachers and schools were seen only on occasion in *The Simpsons, Malcolm in the Middle*, and *Clueless*, and neither the teachers nor the schools were depicted sensitively or positively. Perhaps the most stereotypic depiction of urban schools, teachers, and administrators in recent years was *Boston Public*. Arguably, given the number and frequency of serious problems (drugs, suicide, abuse, sexual imposition, gang activity, shootings, and so on) depicted in one viewing season, *Boston Public* might be seen as a powerful illustration of why *not* to go into teaching, especially in an urban setting.

Again, although we could argue that the teaching profession is at least being noticed and highlighted, we wonder how much respect is being gained through this notice. Mercifully, many of these badly drawn images of teachers and teaching disappear after one or two seasons; but it is troubling that television producers and writers have taken so little effort to depict the teaching profession meaningfully, especially in comparison with the effort put into medical, legal, and police dramas that often feature recognized experts in those fields as either writers or consultants.

Thus, although we have seen an uneven progression toward more serious, mature teachers in school-based books, movies, and television series in the past ten years, on the whole, the images of teachers created by the media still leave much to be desired in terms of authenticity, depth, and variety. Because many adults grew up with the older, more distorted images of teachers and teaching, their perceptions of schools might be quite different than yours. Frequently these more distorted images have found their way into the news media.

SCHOOLS, TEACHERS, AND NEWS IMAGES

In recent years schools and the teaching profession have come under fire by the news media and politicians more than ever before. Much of this fire, of course, can be attributed to a general demystification of all institutions in American society that occurred in the 1960s and 1970s. Nonetheless, the criticisms have seriously eroded the public image of teachers and teaching.

To what extent are these criticisms valid, and what effect have they had on teachers' self-images? Do these emerging images accurately depict the conditions of schools and the skills of teachers? To what degree are recent statements about teachers and teaching reflections of schools that the critics recall from their own childhood rather than of current schools? Why do local papers in small towns frequently present *positive* views of schools in contrast to the views presented by the national news? Which view is more accurate?

NO CHILD LEFT BEHIND (NCLB): THE FEDERAL GOVERNMENT'S IMAGE OF SCHOOLS AND TEACHERS

On January 8, 2002, President George W. Bush signed the No Child Left Behind Act of 2001 (NCLB), which has had a profound impact on teachers and schools across the country. As the centerpiece of President Bush's education reform agenda, it was based on the premise that education should be more inclusive, responsive, and fair (U.S. Department of Education, 2004). Its supporters see it as the national version of the "Texas Miracle" led by then Superintendent of Houston Public Schools Rod Paige, who later became President Bush's secretary of education from 2001 to 2005. Its detractors refer to the act as "no child left untested" and complain about its heavy emphasis on standardized testing for all children throughout the schooling process and the tremendous costs that must be borne by local school districts to meet the requirements of NCLB.

Although NCLB has increased costs to schools, the U.S. Department of Education argues that federal funding to support NCLB requirements has increased significantly as well. The Department of Education points to an $8 billion (46 percent) increase for NCLB programs from 2001 to 2005, a $10.3 billion increase in overall funding for federal elementary and secondary education programs, a $4.6 billion (52 percent) increase for Title I grants for economically disadvantaged students earmarked to be received by local education agencies, and a $4.8 billion (75 percent) increase for grants to states under the Individuals with Disabilities Act (IDEA) Part B (U.S. Department of Education, 2005).

Many of the act's early supporters—including Senator Edward Kennedy, who cosponsored the legislation—are now heavily criticizing both the costs associated with implementing NCLB requirements in local schools and what they perceive as punitive aspects of specific elements of the law. It may be useful to examine some of these elements to determine whether you believe NCLB is a significant effort at educational reform, a boondoggle designed to shake the country's confidence in the ability of public education to truly educate young people, or something in between. As you examine each of the areas of the NCLB law listed in Figure 6.1, try to research each one in more depth by consulting articles, Web sites, and empirical studies done by the U.S. Department of Education, Phi Delta Kappa, and the Center on Education

FIGURE 6.1   Major Provisions of the No Child Left Behind Act of 2001

- *Improving the academic achievement of the economically disadvantaged:* An increase of $1 billion (a 52 percent increase over 2001) for students in high-poverty schools brought the total for Title I programs to $13.3 billion for 2005.

- *Preparing, training, and recruiting highly qualified teachers and principals:* All teachers were to be highly qualified by the end of the 2005–2006 school year. To be highly qualified, a teacher must (1) have a bachelor's degree, (2) hold a certificate/license in the state in which he or she teaches, and (3) have proven knowledge of the subject(s) she or he teaches. The 2005 budget requested $5.1 billion for this area, an increase from $4.4 billion in 2004.

- *Language instruction for limited English proficient and immigrant students:* The president's 2005 budget provided $681 million to fund English language acquisition by children learning the English language.

- *Giving parents choices and creating innovative education programs:* Students in Title I schools that do not make adequate yearly progress, as defined by each state, for two consecutive years can transfer to a higher-performing public school or a charter school within their district. The act added $113 million (increasing the total to $504 million) to help families find schools that best meet their children's needs.

- *Making the education system accountable:* Every state is required to (1) set standards for grade level achievement and (2) develop a system to measure the progress of all students and subgroups of students to meet those standards. The 2006 budget allowed $410 million to support the development and implementation of state assessments to allow parents to compare the performance of each school in their district and across districts.

- *Making the system responsive to local needs:* The act lets local districts transfer up to 50 percent of funds they receive under four major formula grant programs (Teacher Quality State Grants, Educational Technology State Grants, Safe and Drug-Free Schools and Communities State Grants, and State Grants for Innovative Programs) to any one of these programs or to the Title I program for disadvantaged students.

- *Helping all children learn to read:* In the 2005 budget, reading funding increased to a total of $1.4 billion. $1.1 billion was for the Reading First program, with $132 million for the Early Reading First program and $100 million for the Striving Readers program.

- *Helping children with disabilities:* The act includes and extends provisions from the 1997 IDEA Act, which required districtwide and statewide assessments of performance for students with disabilities. Funding increased by $1 billion to a total of $11.1 billion to support children with disabilities.

Policy. Through your own research and discussions of this research in class, determine for yourself how NCLB will impact you as an educator, the school you may teach in, and the district where you currently live.

After you research, analyze, and discuss the major provisions of the NCLB Act of 2001, interview local teachers and school administrators to determine if this law has had any specific or general impact on them. As you consider their responses, identify how this law might affect you as you prepare to become a teacher, and how it might affect you after you begin your first teaching job.

THE IMAGE OF EDUCATION AND THE NEWS MEDIA

Although the No Child Left Behind Act may have created the impression that U.S. public schools are in serious trouble and need significant repair, this is not a new attack on public education. At various times during the past century, schools have been criticized for being too liberal, too repressive, too factorylike, too open and unstructured, and too status quo oriented. High schools, in particular, have been the target of major concern—from the Committee of Ten in the late 1890s to the Coleman Report in the late 1960s to the recent criticism leveled by the Bill and Melinda Gates Foundation at the 2005 National Governors Conference.

Although public schools and teachers have been the subject of severe criticism here and there during the past century, the quantity and intensity of that criticism have increased significantly since 1983 when the book *A Nation at Risk: The Imperative for Educational Reform* was published by the U.S. Department of Education as a report of the National Commission on Excellence in Education. This report gained considerable national attention and press when it referred to the "rising tide of mediocrity" in U.S. schools and implied that if a foreign power had made our public schools' students perform as badly as they did on national assessments, we would consider it an act of war (National Commission on Excellence in Education, 1983). The use of this type of hyperbolic rhetoric in a report sponsored by the federal government served as a catalyst for a plethora of similar reports by organizations, foundations, and of course, the news media that still come out regularly.

To what extent are these reports, their allegations, and the subsequent public outcry warranted? In 1997 David C. Berliner and Bruce J. Biddle addressed many of these issues in their book *The Manufactured Crisis*. The Berliner and Biddle book was published when education was receiving severe criticism for not even being close to attaining the outcomes identified in the Goals 2000 mandate nearly eight years after those goals were articulated by a bipartisan panel of governors and federal officials. Has the image of schools and teachers, and education in general, changed since 1997? If so, is that image more positive? Are the concerns raised by Berliner and Biddle "old news," or are they still relevant issues today?

In the Core Activity of this chapter, a selection of these issues are listed. Research and discuss each of the statements in the activity and determine whether you believe the statements are facts or myths. Then consult *The Manufactured Crisis* to determine whether Berliner and Biddle believe these statements are facts or myths. Finally, discuss whether you believe Berliner and Biddle are correct in their analysis of these statements. After this activity is completed, discuss in your Journal Entry for this chapter the degree to which you believe the image of schools and teachers depicted in the news media is accurate and represents your image of schools and teachers.

Core Activity

STATEMENTS ABOUT SCHOOLS AND TEACHERS
(SOURCE: *THE MANUFACTURED CRISIS*, 1997)

1. Student achievement has recently fallen across the nation.

   Myth   Fact

   Reason:

   _____

   _____

   _____

   _____

2. American schools fail in comparative studies (with other industrialized nations) of student achievement.

   Myth   Fact

   Reason:

   _____

   _____

   _____

   _____

3. America spends a lot more money on education than other countries.

   Myth   Fact

   Reason:

   _____

   _____

   _____

   _____

4. Money is not related to school achievement.

                        Myth   Fact

Reason:

_____

_____

_____

_____

5. Costs in education have recently skyrocketed wastefully.

                        Myth   Fact

Reason:

_____

_____

_____

_____

6. American public schools and textbooks no longer promote moral values.

                        Myth   Fact

Reason:

_____

_____

_____

_____

7. American citizens are unhappy with their schools.

                        Myth   Fact

Reason:

_____

_____

_____

_____

8. Private schools are inherently better than public schools.

                         Myth   Fact

Reason:

_____

_____

_____

_____

Are the teachers you are observing well respected by students, parents, and others?

"I would appreciate it very much if you wouldn't hum the tune from 'The Twilight Zone' every time I enter the classroom!"

Originally published in Phi Delta Kappan

By now you may have concluded that overall the teacher's image is rather shaky both within the profession and nationally. Although there is some validity to that conclusion, it doesn't mean that this image is the whole story; there are more positives in the image than are generally recognized. Therefore, part of your growth as a teacher will involve confronting the issues of image versus substance, myth versus reality, and opinion versus fact. In the following activities you can explore the nature of teacher image and its effect on teaching and schools. From your explorations, you can draw conclusions supported by facts, realities, and substance. This will let you discover that (1) society is deeply indebted to teachers and (2) many teachers feel good about their decision to enter teaching. Along the way you may recollect a teacher who helped you out when you were upset or in a personal crisis. You may also find that teachers have many sources of joy as well as of frustration. Finally, you may learn that part of the challenge of becoming a teacher is learning to be yourself rather than fitting or overcoming an image that is neither accurate nor real.

Suggested Activity 1

MY MOST INFLUENTIAL TEACHER(S)

As you were directly experiencing teachers and schools during your childhood and adolescence, you were probably influenced considerably by your interactions with these teachers or with family friends who were (are) teachers. In addition, you were exposed to a variety of media models on television and in movies and books. These models also influenced your perceptions of teachers and teaching. In the spaces that follow, describe the characteristics and behaviors (positive and negative) of these teachers and the media models that you were exposed to and briefly discuss how your perceptions of teachers and teaching were influenced. Please note that *your* influential teacher could be a media figure like Sidney Poitier (*To Sir with Love*) or Michelle Pfeiffer (*Dangerous Minds*) or could be a real teacher whom you experienced in your own school career.

THE TEACHER(S) I WOULD *MOST* LIKELY EMULATE

Characteristics:

_____

_____

_____

_____

Behaviors:

_____

_____

_____

_____

THE TEACHER(S) I WOULD *LEAST* LIKELY EMULATE

Characteristics:

_____

_____

_____

_____

Behaviors:

_____

_____

_____

_____

Suggested Activity 2

MEDIA ROLE MODELS

Briefly discuss how your ideas about teaching were influenced by the characteristics of the teacher models listed next.

1. Movie roles:
   Male

   _____

   _____

   _____

   Female

   _____

   _____

   _____

2. Television roles:
   Male

   _____

   _____

   _____

   Female

   _____

   _____

   _____

3. Literary roles:
   Male

   _____

   _____

   _____

   Female

   _____

   _____

   _____

Suggested Activity 3

HOW DOES YOUR TEACHER FEEL ABOUT TEACHING?

In the previous activities you examined your own images of teachers and teaching, some of which were derived from direct experiences and some from media models. In this activity you will continue to apply your interviewing skills in a structured interview with the teacher whom you are observing and with other teachers with whom you may have contact. Besides the questions suggested next, feel free to incorporate some of your own based on your observations and class discussions.

1. Did any teachers you had in school influence your decision to enter teaching? In what ways did they influence you?

2. Did you seek to emulate any behaviors or characteristics of these teachers when you entered teaching? What are some examples of these behaviors or characteristics?

3. What do you perceive to be the public image of teachers in American society today? Is this image accurate or misleading? In what ways?

4. Do movies, TV, and novels depict teachers accurately or stereotypically?

5. Did you find any media role models of teachers to be particularly gratifying? For example, consider Sidney Poitier (*To Sir with Love*), Gabe Kaplan (*Welcome Back Kotter*), Richard Dreyfuss (*Mr. Holland's Opus*), William Hurt (*Children of a Lesser God*), Robin Williams (*Dead Poet's Society*), and Edward James Olmos (*Stand and Deliver*).

6. Did you find any media role models of teachers to be particularly disheartening? For example, consider the study hall supervisor in *Breakfast Club*, Ichabod Crane, and Mr. Hand in *Fast Times at Ridgemont High*.

7. How do local newspapers contribute to your community's perception of local teachers? Do they portray teachers in a positive light?

8. Do you feel that you have to maintain one image in school and/or with parents and another image in your private life? Does that create any difficulties for you?

9. In what ways has the teacher's image changed since you began teaching? What are your feelings about those changes?

ADDITIONAL QUESTIONS

1. From your data, what conclusions can you draw about teachers' perceptions of teacher image?

_____

_____

_____

_____

2. How do these perceptions compare with your own?

_____

_____

_____

_____

_____

Student Name: _____   Date: _____

Journal Entry

Because this chapter concentrated on teacher image and how that image has evolved, your Journal Entry here should concentrate on your perceptions of teachers and teaching and how you arrived at your perceptions. Within this Journal Entry, you should elaborate on the feelings you had when you

1. Interviewed teachers about their perceptions of teacher image.
2. Considered the role that media play in shaping your and the public's image of teachers.
3. Listened to your class members discuss their findings about recent criticisms of teachers and schools.
4. Reflected on your own decision to enter teaching and the kind of public image that you would like to create as a teacher.

_____

_____

_____

_____

_____

_____

_____

_____

_____

_____

_____

_____

_____

_____

Questions for Discussion

1. How critical is the public's image of teachers and teaching to your decision to enter teaching?

2. How could teachers improve their image with the public? Suggest some strategies that school districts, teachers' organizations, or student teacher groups might employ to attain this improvement.

3. Some critics have suggested that teachers create two images—one that reflects their public selves and one that reflects their private selves. Based on your observations, interviews, and class discussions, analyze the extent to which teachers create two distinct images.

4. Given your analyses of the media models of teachers, discuss how these models create stereotypes of the teaching profession and how they may create public expectations that are difficult for teachers to attain.

5. Describe your "ideal" teacher and the sources (real teachers, media models, etc.) that you drew upon to create this image.

References

Berliner, D. C., and Biddle, B. J. (1997). *The manufactured crisis: Myths, fraud, and the attack on America's public schools* (pp. 13–125). White Plains, NY: Longman Publishers.

Endrst, James. (1996, October 6). Putting a grade on TV's 5 new school series. *The Toledo Blade, TV Week*, 3.

Feistritzer, E. C. (1985). *The condition of teaching: A state by state analysis* (pp. 69–72, 92–95). Princeton, NJ: Princeton University Press.

Gates's $2.3 billion revamping the three R's. (2005, May 16). *Toledo Blade*.

Husen, Torsten. (1983, March). Are standards in U.S. schools really lagging behind those in other countries? *Phi Delta Kappan*, 455–461.

National Commission on Excellence in Education. (1983). *A nation at risk: The imperative for school reform*. Washington, DC: author.

Sizer, T. (1984). *Horace's compromise: The dilemma of the American high school*. Boston: Houghton Mifflin.

U.S. Department of Education. (2004). *A guide to education and No Child Left Behind*. Washington, DC: Office of the Secretary, Office of Public Affairs.

U.S. Department of Education. (2005, March). *No Child Left Behind: Expanding the promise. A guide to President Bush's FY 2006 education agenda*. Washington, DC. Web site: http://www.ed.gov/about/overview/budget/budget06/nclb/index.html.

Welcome Back Kotter teacher named TV's most memorable. Retrieved September 1, 2005, from http://www.HoustonChronicle.com.

Williams, D. A. (1985, September). Why teachers fail. *Newsweek*, 64–66.

Chapter 7

THE SCHOOL AND ITS COMMUNITY

Once upon a time, there were no schools. People learned everything from their family or tribe or from the hard lessons of direct experience. Most of what was to be learned was survival skills: how to hunt and trap, how to keep the fire going, how to find good water. Poor or slow learners usually had short lives, both individually and as communities. Experience was, indeed, a harsh teacher.

As time progressed, some tribal communities developed more skills and had more to pass on to their young. Increasingly, too, it seemed inefficient for everyone to do everything. It became clear that people had different talents, different contributions to the welfare of the community. Some could build; some could hunt; some could lead. The human community discovered specialization of labor. The accumulation of knowledge and skills, plus the specialization of labor, is tightly linked to the history of education. At a certain point in the evolution of a human community it became inefficient for parents to spend so much time teaching their children. The education of Alexander the Great is an example. Alexander's father, Philip of Macedon, was too busy ruling and extending his empire to teach his son all that Philip knew Alexander would need to know to follow in his footsteps, so Philip hired the wisest man he knew to teach his son. He hired Aristotle, and the great Greek philosopher became the personal tutor of the young man who was to conquer and rule all of the known world.

But as this example suggests, formal education was a luxury reserved for the elite. In the Roman Empire wealthy families often had teachers who were slaves captured from far-off lands. Later the church began schools, usually attached to monasteries. These often evolved into universities, where knowledge was collected, copied, codified, and passed on. Royal courts began to hire teachers. Later the wealthy merchant classes hired tutors, and they established small schools for their children. But in all these examples schooling was a social luxury reserved for those who would eventually lead the community in some way: as a ruler, as a churchman, as a merchant, or, to continue the line, as a scholar–teacher. Schools served the social elite and only indirectly the rest of the community.

Schooling was a major factor in the development of the New World. In colonial New England, Puritan parents believed that it was important for children to be able to read the Bible and thus to protect themselves from Satan. On the other hand, they were too busy eking out a living from the cold rocky soil of New England to teach their children themselves. They decided to establish schools and in 1647 passed the

Old Deluder Act.* This historic act set the pattern for community-supported schools. It required that every town of fifty or more families pay a man to teach the children to read and write. From these beginnings, schools spread across the continent. As knowledge and skills developed and as the demands of commerce and an ever more complex business world emerged, schools snowballed. Instead of education being the province of the rulers and the wealthy, it spread to everyone. More children began to go to school for longer periods. Grades and levels of schooling were established. Grammar schools were followed by high schools.

Following the pattern set in New England, communities saw that it was in their best interest to require education. So education became compulsory, and it continued to require more time in the lives of children. Also, the specialization of labor that originally led to the selection of certain people as teachers (to be, in effect, culture carriers) created increasing specialization among teachers. As communities wanted more material taught, it became clear that specialization was needed *within* teaching—so we now educate elementary teachers who specialize in the primary grades, physics teachers for advanced students, and so on. It is a safe wager that both of these trends—more education for more people and more specialization within teaching—will increase.

Schools, then, developed as a direct result of community needs and sometimes community demands. As such, they reflect what a community believes it needs to survive. In times of rapid social and technological changes (like the present) schools represent what people think their children will need to live successful lives and to maintain the community in the future. And communities make very different choices. For example, the Amish communities in the Midwest have rejected much recent technological progress and its values. As a result, their schools teach the Bible and the basics and shun much of the literature, science, mathematics and vocational programs that are taught in modern schools.

One of the most distinctive features of the American system of education is the relationship between schools and their communities. We have a highly decentralized school system, which gives a local community an enormous range of choice in how it structures schools and what it teaches its children. Most other modern nations, like Russia and France, are quite centralized. The minister of education in Moscow or Paris says what will be taught in the third grade or in the eleventh grade throughout the country. The minister of education, in effect, represents all of the people and one set of choices about what children will need. In our country we have approximately 15,000 centers of education power: 15,000 school districts, boards of education, superintendents of schools. And unlike Russia and France, which in effect make one social gamble about schools, we make 15,000 different gambles.

Although this decentralized nature of American schools is one of our nation's distinguishing marks, there are all sorts of pressures to encourage commonalities among our schools. Among these common elements are textbooks, important examinations such as the SATs and ACTs, and nationwide professional associations such as the National Education Association and the Association for Supervision and Curriculum Development. These and other forces influence decision makers in our 15,000 school districts to consider similar issues and choose similar solutions. Like much in American society, our schools are influenced by a strong sense of competition.

---

*The act was named for the primary reason for the establishment of schools: to teach children to read the Bible, thus arming them against the snares and temptations of Satan, the "Old Deluder."

The stakes of this educational wager are high—whether we are talking about neighboring communities in this nation or competing nations. Few communities are exactly of one mind about what their future citizens will need; thus decisions about school systems are frequently heated, with different groups wanting different kinds of programs. What finally gets taught is the result not only of the accumulation of knowledge and skills, but also of a political process, the struggle of a community over a classic education question: "What is most worth knowing?" Math and science? How to get along with others? Critical thinking skills and the tools of learning? Character development and moral values? How much emphasis should be placed on each of these priorities? Not long ago Joseph Macekura, a longtime Virginia educator, stated,

> A school is the child of the community—fathered and mothered by all of the dreams and hopes, and bred by the frustration and hopelessness, in the hearts of its citizens . . . society's expectation of a school is an ever-expanding one. Like an expanding ripple in a pond created by a tossed stone, each ripple in society envelops yet another demand for the school. Where chaos exists, schools are expected to create order. Where confusion and anger exist, schools are expected to calm group and individual upheavals and substitute hope. Where individual abuse and degradation leave their indelible scars, schools are expected to regenerate, like crayfish, a new appendage of healing and stability.

In a sense, then, schools are under pressure to be all things to all people, which is another way to say that they are frequently caught in the cross fire of a community's differing dreams and goals.

In general, though, schools tend to reflect the dominant values of their communities. In effect, we get what we pay for. But even in the best of situations, there are tensions between the school and its community. Communities do not have one voice. Not only are there often competing goals; some people, such as those with no children or children out of school, may not be particularly interested in schools.

Another source of tension is related to the one just mentioned. Many people may have different priorities for their tax dollars than schools, or "youth ghettoes," as they are sometimes called by nonsupporters. In the last few decades in this country we have seen a large swing in population and social priorities from school and youth development to medical insurance and the aged. Often people with young children and those who have no children in schools disagree over how much should be spent on children.

A third source of tension is the relationship between what schools are currently doing and what the community wants them to do. A school board member may voice a widespread concern for better student writing, but it may take several years to retrain and hire teachers and set in place a successful language arts program; and until the program begins reaping tangible results and the community notices those results, there will be strains. It is not uncommon, too, that by the time the school has reacted positively to the community's will, there are new board members with new priorities: Exit writing, and enter emphasis on technological skills or the arts.

This within-community tension over educational aims has emerged recently under the guise of a desire for "school choice." While we have always had school choice in the form of vibrant private and religious schools, this has been a school choice that not everyone could afford. In recent years new voices have been calling for greater choice within public schools, such as charter schools and using public funds to support private and religious schools. Currently several states are experimenting with various "voucher plans" typically aimed at giving poor parents an educational

How much of the quality of education in a community is a reflection of what the community values and supports politically?

"Aid to education sounds fine, but you and I know what will happen if the voters get too damned bright."

Holt, Rinehart and Winston

voucher to purchase nonpublic schooling for their children. Finally, another indication of within-community tension is the popularity of homeschooling. In the 2004–2005 school year 1,100,000 students were being homeschooled in this country. Frequently the choice to homeschool is driven by dissatisfaction with the social climate in local public schools or parents' desire to provide religious education for their children.

A fourth source of tension is between particular groups within the school community. Often parents with serious academic aspirations for their children may be at odds with what they perceive as the schools' "social adjustment" emphasis or their emphasis on sports. Sometimes working-class parents feel that the schools are giving too much attention to preparation for college and not taking seriously their non-college-bound students. Differences may become so aggravated that parents move and put their children into another public school or a private school. Again, this generally is a luxury that only the rich and the middle class can afford. The poor are stuck with the schools in their community and rarely can move to search for better education.

A fifth source of tension exists naturally between parents and those who have a hand in raising their children. Teachers have a different function than parents. Teachers see the child in a different, more public light. Their focus is usually narrower, dealing with a child's cognitive skills and social personality. They seldom see the private side of the child. They do not see the child embedded in a family network of events and aspirations. Teachers have only a slice of the child's life and lack the child's history, a history that the parents know intimately. Some years ago Boston-based columnist Ellen Goodman wrote about her feelings as her daughter was graduating from the eighth grade. Her reflections lay bare some of the tensions that exist between the school and community members:

> The mother had brought her daughter to this school with the usual baggage of mixed emotions. She signed the girl up for learning and turned over her hours and control. Her daughter was, largely, set on her own.
>
> At times the two—parents and teachers, families and schools—formed an alliance. At times they had similar visions; at times quite the opposite. But together they made a life.
>
> From the first day to this, the last day, the mother had felt moments of uncertainty and distance from the school. On occasion she had overreacted, underreacted, misjudged events she hadn't witnessed.
>
> At times, the girl must have felt as if she were in shared custody. She uttered lines that sounded like captions for missing pictures: "But that's what the teacher told me. All the kids are doing it. You don't understand."
>
> After eight years, the mother was no longer surprised by any tension that existed between parents and schools.
>
> Even the best of schools frame another world for our children, hurt them, reward them, test them by other standards. Even the best schools separate them from us, give them other adults, other rules, other ideas.*

Even neighboring communities in this country have different educational systems. One community will tax itself heavily for its schools. The other won't, stressing instead recreation or programs for the elderly or letting people keep their money. One community may emphasize math and science throughout its schools; another school may focus on foreign language; yet another on physical education. At present, some communities are making a heavy investment in teaching computer literacy, whereas others are sticking to the "tried and true," concluding that computers are a passing fancy. As we have said, what is taught in school is a social bet, a particular community's wager concerning what its children will need to live well in the future.

The relationship between a school and its community is complicated. Although everyone wants children to have a good education, there are enormous differences of opinion about what constitutes a good education. Although everyone wants good schools, not everyone wants to pay for good schools. And although it may not appear so on the surface, public schools in the United States are heavily involved in the push-and-pull of the democratic process. Although school board elections rarely involve party politics, they are political events in which the people directly elect candidates whose educational views they find most compatible with their own.

Thomas "Tip" O'Neill, a famous Speaker of the House of Representatives in the 1980s, once commented on national politics with the statement, "All politics is local

---

Boston Globe, July 8, 1982.

politics." The elected public official who forgets this is usually soon unemployed. The same is true of school board members and the school superintendent: They cannot get too far from the wishes of the community they serve. This makes American schools accountable to local citizens, who not only elect the school policy makers—the board—but who also control the schools' purse strings by regularly deciding how much they are willing to tax themselves to pay for education.

We have mentioned that American schools are distinctive in their decentralized control. Elected local school boards and heavy dependence on local taxing are key to that decentralization. As opposed to countries with centralized control by a minister of education who makes decisions from the nation's capital, our schools are close to the people. They are both accountable to the community and vulnerable to community discontent. One manifestation of this vulnerability is the high turnover rate among superintendents of schools.

We have emphasized the political nature of schools and the tensions that can exist in a community over schools to prepare you to look more critically at the schools, the school system, and the community in which you are observing. To understand what goes on inside a school, it is often necessary to understand what goes on outside that school. It is important to know the community in which a school is embedded. To help you do this, we have developed and selected a number of activities.

Core Activity
YOUR SCHOOL/COMMUNITY IQ

Schools are a major part of a community. They are bound to their particular community by seen and unseen bonds, by past achievements and future hopes. Particularly in the United States, where schools are decentralized and controlled locally, the link between schools and community is strong. To know your school, you need to know your community. To know your community, you need to know your school.

You will probably be surprised by how much information is known about individual schools and how readily available it is. Everything from scores on recent statewide tests to today's cafeteria menu is just a few clicks away on the Internet. Before you go further in this Core Activity, you first should do a warm-up activity. Spend fifteen minutes on the Internet reacquainting yourself with your own junior high or middle school. Find the school's Web site by going to either the city or town's Web site or the Web site of the school district; from there, link to the school's Web site. Now answer the following questions:

1. How many of my old teachers are still there?
2. Is the science curriculum still the same? What about social studies?
3. Check out the school's mission statement or statement of philosophy. Does it describe your educational experience there?
4. What is the school doing that is new and interesting?
5. Are they still serving the same food in the cafeteria?

Next check out two other middle schools in different parts of the country. Two possibilities are Brown Middle School in Newton, Massachusetts, a suburb of Boston [http://www.newton. mec.edu/Brown/], and Corwin Middle School in Pueblo, Colorado [http://www.pueblo60.k12. co.us/corwin.nsf]. Spend ten minutes inspecting each site and answer the following questions:

1. Which of these two middle schools would you rather attend? Why?
2. How are the academic programs similar? How are they different?
3. In your judgment, which offers the richer educational environment?
4. Can you make any "educated guesses" about the social makeup of these two communities? Can you find evidence for your conclusions from other sources on the Internet?
5. How does your middle school or junior high compare with these schools?

The next part of this exercise will let you test how much you actually know about a particular community and its schools. Work with either your home schools and their community or the school and community in which you are currently observing. If you are in doubt about which to use, check with your instructor.

This test will confront you with issues that you may never have considered or for which you do not have answers. Where you do not have a ready answer, try to think it through. Where you do not have exact information, make an educated guess.

Student Name: _____   Date: _____

THE COMMUNITY

1. If an interested friend asked you to describe this community, what are some things that you would tell him or her? Like a good reporter, try to be as detailed as possible in your answer.

_____

_____

_____

_____

_____

_____

_____

_____

_____

_____

_____

_____

_____

_____

_____

_____

_____

_____

_____

_____

_____

_____

_____

_____

2. What is the approximate population of your community? _____ people

3. How large is your community? _____ miles wide; _____ miles long

4. What are the major sources of income of the people in your community?

   a. _____

   b. _____

   c. _____

   d. _____

   e. _____

   f. _____

5. Estimate the percentage of the working population in each of the following occupational groups:

   _____% Type 1—small business owner

   _____% Type 2—skilled worker (secretary, nurse's aide, technician)

   _____% Type 3—professional (doctor, lawyer, architect)

   _____% Type 4—public servant (politician, government worker)

   _____% Type 5—teacher or others involved in education

   _____% Type 6—laborer (factory worker)

   _____% Type 7—tradesperson (plumber, carpenter, machinist)

   _____% Type 8—business executive, management, salesperson

   _____% Type 9—farmer

   _____% Type 10—homemaker

   _____% Type 11—other (specify) _____

6. What percentage of the adult women work outside the home? _____ %

7. What is your estimate of the major religious groups in your community?

   _____% Protestant

   _____% Catholic

   _____% Jewish

   _____% Other (specify) _____

8. List the percentages of these groups in your community:

_____ % White Americans

_____ % Black Americans

_____ % Asian Americans

_____ % Hispanic Americans

_____ % Other (specify) _____

9. List and estimate the percentages of the major ethnic and/or national groups in your community.

_____ % _____

_____ % _____

_____ % _____

_____ % _____

_____ % _____

10. How would you describe the current state of your community? As a vital, growing community? As an old, but still vital, community? As a slowly decaying community? Describe in your own words what you believe to be the health of your community.

_____

_____

_____

_____

_____

_____

_____

_____

11. What percentage of people in your community are newcomers? _____ %
Do people in this community refer to newcomers as "outsiders"? _____
What percentage of the people in the community would you estimate have attended the local schools? _____ %

12. In your judgment, is your community a good place for young people to grow up? Why or why not?

_____

_____

_____

_____

_____

_____

_____

13. Visit a police station and ask an officer to describe the crime situation in the community (e.g., major crimes, most frequent crimes). Ask in particular about youth crimes and specifically about drug use, underage drinking, and gang activities.

_____

_____

_____

_____

_____

_____

_____

_____

14. Thinking broadly about education in your community, list the educational institutions where learning goes on. Do not confine yourself to the public and private schools.

a. _____

b. _____

c. _____

d. _____

e. _____

f. _____

g. _____

h. _____

i. _____

j. _____

k. _____

l. _____

m. _____

n. _____

o. _____

p. _____

q. _____

r. _____

s. _____

t. _____

15. Is there competition among any of these institutions? If so, how would you describe it?

_____

_____

_____

_____

_____

_____

_____

_____

_____

_____

_____

_____

_____

_____

YOUR SCHOOL

1. In general, do you believe that teachers in your community are respected? Why or why not?

_____

_____

_____

_____

_____

_____

_____

2. Where do the teachers reside in the community?

   _____% live in the community.

   _____% live outside the community.

3. What percentage of teachers attended the local elementary and secondary schools when they were young? _____ %

4. On average, do teachers make as much money as the majority of people in the community? _____

5. How would you describe the relationship between the teachers whom you know well and the people in the community?

_____

_____

_____

_____

_____

_____

_____

_____

6. What evidence do you see of teachers drawing upon the resources, both personal and institutional, of the community?

_____

_____

_____

_____

_____

_____

_____

_____

_____

_____

_____

_____

7. Summarize your views on the relationships among the school, the teachers, and the community.

_____

_____

_____

_____

_____

_____

_____

_____

_____

8. How would you describe your own attitudes toward this community? Is it a place where you would like to teach? Is it a place where you would like to live?

_____

_____

_____

_____

_____

_____

_____

_____

_____

_____

_____

_____

_____

_____

Note: If you had trouble filling out this school/community questionnaire, you may wish to get some help. The Internet is probably the best place to start. Then there is city hall or town hall, often a good source of general information about a community. So, too, are the local newspapers and the chamber of commerce. Because it is important for school administrators to know their community, they often have at their fingertips much of the kind of information requested here. Finally, the teachers and administrators in the school in which you are observing may be another source of information and insight to help you answer these questions.

Student Name: _____   Date: _____

Suggested Activity 1

COMMUNITY MEMBER INTERVIEW

In this activity get the views of three community members (ideally, one should be a school board member) on the following questions:

1. How would you describe the community's support for its schools?
   Community member 1:

   _____

   _____

   _____

   _____

   _____

   _____

   Community member 2:

   _____

   _____

   _____

   _____

   _____

   _____

   Community member 3:

   _____

   _____

   _____

   _____

   _____

   _____

2. How would you describe the community's willingness to pay for good schools?
   Community member 1:

   _____

   _____

   _____

   _____

   _____

   _____

   _____

   Community member 2:

   _____

   _____

   _____

   _____

   _____

   _____

   _____

   Community member 3:

   _____

   _____

   _____

   _____

   _____

   _____

   _____

3. What aspects of the schools tend to be most heavily supported, or what is most favorably viewed by the community?

Community member 1:

_____

_____

_____

_____

_____

_____

_____

Community member 2:

_____

_____

_____

_____

_____

_____

Community member 3:

_____

_____

_____

_____

_____

_____

4. What are the strongest criticisms that are heard about the schools from community members?

Community member 1:

_____

_____

_____

_____

_____

_____

_____

Community member 2:

_____

_____

_____

_____

_____

_____

_____

Community member 3:

_____

_____

_____

_____

_____

_____

_____

Student Name: _____ Date: _____

Suggested Activity 2

EDUCATOR INTERVIEW

Pick three educators (ideally an experienced teacher, a new teacher, and an administrator) from the school in which you are observing and ask them the following questions:

1. How would you describe this community's support for its schools?
   Educator 1:

   _____

   _____

   _____

   _____

   _____

   _____

   _____

   Educator 2:

   _____

   _____

   _____

   _____

   _____

   _____

   _____

   Educator 3:

   _____

   _____

   _____

   _____

_____

_____

_____

2. How would you describe this community's willingness to pay for good schools?
   Educator 1:

_____

_____

_____

_____

_____

Educator 2:

_____

_____

_____

_____

_____

Educator 3:

_____

_____

_____

_____

_____

3. What aspects of a school tend to be most heavily supported, or what is most favorably viewed by this community?

Educator 1:

_____

_____

_____

_____

_____

_____

Educator 2:

_____

_____

_____

_____

_____

_____

Educator 3:

_____

_____

_____

_____

_____

_____

4. What are the strongest criticisms that are heard about the schools from community members?

Educator 1:

_____

_____

_____

_____

_____

_____

Educator 2:

_____

_____

_____

_____

_____

_____

Educator 3:

_____

_____

_____

_____

_____

_____

_____

Student Name: _____   Date: _____

Suggested Activity 3
TRUTH OR EXAGGERATION?

Social conditions change, and so do schools. What a community expects or demands of its schools shifts with new social priorities. Not long ago a group of educators in Ohio wrote the following mock job opening announcement. The job description tells a lot about the realities of teaching but also exaggerates a great deal.

As you read this pretend "Personnel Wanted" advertisement, underline what you feel are exaggerations and put checkmarks next to the more realistic points.

PERSONNEL WANTED
Openings are available in a variety of areas for special people. Are you in a rut? No variety in your present position? Are you a professional-type person who loves children and a challenge? Check the following requirements and see if you qualify.

QUALIFICATIONS
At least a bachelor's degree (with an average of two additional years of college work).

You should also be . . . loving . . . arts/craftsy . . . athletic . . . resourceful . . . understanding . . . creative . . . loyal . . . enthusiastic . . . organized . . . dependable . . . knowledgeable . . . responsible to leadership . . . aware of fads . . . committed . . . able to update antiquated materials . . . accountable . . . fair disciplinarian . . . unfailingly cheerful . . . well-read . . . respectful . . . alert . . . quick decision maker . . . willing volunteer . . . multitalented . . . wise . . . charismatic . . . psychic . . . trivia expert . . . mechanically inclined . . . able to please everyone all of the time . . . honest . . . strong in nerves . . . sensitive . . . tactful . . . mentally and physically healthy . . . diplomatic . . . fair . . . diverse interests . . . well-informed . . . patient . . . attractive . . . unflappable . . . superhuman in stamina . . . not easily frustrated . . . able to enunciate . . . physically strong . . . community oriented . . . able to function in crisis situations . . . ABLE TO TEACH!

FURTHER REQUIREMENTS
You must be able to . . .

keep records . . . collect money . . . coach . . . support school functions (monetarily) . . . plan a curriculum . . . write behavioral objectives . . . write lesson plans . . . write reports of all kinds . . . attend seminars, athletic events, plays, carnivals, festivals, musicals, fund-raising events, parent–teacher organization meetings, graduations, committee meetings, school board meetings, department meetings, faculty meetings.

And be able to . . .

supervise lunchroom, recess, halls, bathrooms, study hall, detention, assemblies, plays, student council . . . prepare infallible testing instruments, create the perfect testing environment . . . evaluate all work . . . provide guidance . . . break up fights . . . check students for drugs and/or alcohol . . . deal with discipline . . . maintain a quiet classroom . . . interpret medical records.

Must be a(n) . . .

   secretary . . . adviser . . . photographer . . . ticket   taker . . . librarian . . . curriculum   developer . . . veterinarian . . . plumber . . . mechanic . . . biologist . . . handwriting   expert . . . typist . . . interior   decorator . . . entertainer . . . lecturer . . .   janitor . . . carpenter . . . electrician . . . diagnostician . . . chauffeur . . . chaperone . . . nurse . . . statistician . . . dishwasher . . . housekeeper . . . psychiatrist . . . confidant . . . leader . . . cook . . . host/hostess . . . mathematician . . . historian . . . nutritionist . . . politician . . . accountant . . . linguist . . . cryptologist . . . author . . . companion . . . friend . . . file   clerk . . . office   machines   expert . . . tear-dryer . . . hand holder . . . back patter . . . shoulder lender . . . ego builder . . . shoe tier . . . nose wiper . . . boot tugger . . . clothes zipper . . . lost book finder . . . problem solver . . . father/mother confessor . . . lovelorn adviser.

WORKING CONDITIONS

- One book, chair, and desk you may have to share (the desk doesn't lock).
- Poor lighting, heating, and circulation.
- Inadequate restroom and medical facilities.
- Infrequent or nonexistent breaks with the exception of forty minutes for lunch and calls of a personal nature.
- Institutional food (if you have the time and/or appetite).

FRINGE BENEFITS

- All the gum you can scrape off the bottoms of desks.
- A growing collection of broken pencils, confiscated squirt guns, and miscellaneous animals, insects, and reptiles.
- Vocabulary development (you will learn many new words).
- Exposure to original graffiti and love letters.
- More free advice than you can use.
- Opportunity to move from assignment to assignment; from class to class; from school to school.
- High esteem in your community.
- Exposure to various pathogens.

If you feel you have the qualifications, if you love a challenge, contact your local school board office for an application.

Student Name: _____   Date: _____

Journal Entry

Your observation and study of your current school should focus on the relationship between the school and the community that it is serving and by which it is being supported. In this Journal Entry consider (but don't necessarily write about) the following questions and issues:

1. What tensions exist between the school and the community?
2. What attitudes toward this community's children have you detected from residents and from teachers?
3. To what degree are the teachers "of the community"? Are they similar, socially and educationally, to the majority of the parents whose children they teach? Do they live in the community? Do they reflect the values of the community?
4. What aspects of the school program (sports, dramatics, vocational programs, foreign language programs) receive a good deal of support from the community?
5. What is the evidence that the community financially supports the school? What is the physical condition of the school? Does the school have an adequate gym? Auditorium? Library? Computer labs? How does the teacher salary scale compare with that of communities around it?

_____

_____

_____

_____

_____

_____

_____

_____

_____

_____

_____

_____

Questions for Discussion

1. If schools were to disappear, along with the very idea of schooling, what other ways might we invent to prepare the young for adulthood?

2. How would the life of your family be changed if its members were responsible for the bulk of your education? What would be gained, and what would be lost?

3. Selecting either the school/community in which you are currently observing or your "home" school/community (the one that you know best), discuss the major tensions that exist between the school and the community.

4. What are some things that teachers, administrators, and students can do to strengthen the bonds between students and their communities?

Chapter 8

HUMOR IN THE CLASSROOM

Are classrooms a rich source for identifying humorous incidents? Do teachers who use humor extensively appear to be more effective than those who don't? Do students at different ages view humor differently? Are there gender differences that affect the use of humor in the classroom? Does the use of humor increase student retention and achievement? Is it possible to "plan" humor into lessons? These questions, among many others, have been posed by researchers seeking to determine if humor has a place in schools.

Research on humor in teaching has emerged only recently. Most of the research has occurred during the past twenty-five years and has yielded mixed results (Neulip, 1991). Much of the empirical research has been done with college students, so the conclusions have only marginal applications to teaching strategies at the elementary and secondary level. Because of concerns over reducing test anxiety, a number of studies looked at the use of humor in creating test items for a variety of objective tests (multiple choice, true–false, matching, etc.: Vance, 1987; Ziv, 1988). In general, studies of application-oriented discussions of humor in the classroom stress the need to use humor judiciously, occasionally, and in a developmentally appropriate manner with a concerted effort to make it as relevant as possible to the topic at hand (McGhee, 1971; Gorham and Christophel, 1990). Furthermore, at least one synthesis of research on effective thinking includes the ability to find what is humorous in a given situation as one of the sixteen essential habits of mind (Costa and Kallick, 2000).

Trying to analyze humor to determine what makes people laugh usually results in mixed reactions from readers. Part of this is due to the fact that humor is frequently derived from situational variables that are uniquely funny ("You had to be there"). It also assumes that the reader has developed the appropriate mental setting to understand the humor ("I don't get it."). Finally, what the humor analyst believes to be intensely funny may simply be lost on the reader who has different tastes ("I don't like puns, slapstick, off-color jokes, visual humor," etc.). In trying to provide examples to illustrate types of humor that occur in classrooms, or in trying to describe how teachers can use humor effectively, any or all of the conditions just identified could come into play. However, this shouldn't dissuade you from trying to identify humorous aspects of teaching, extracurricular work with students, or simply dealing with bureaucratic irrationality in and outside the classroom. Your success in making these identifications will relate to how well you understand your own sense of humor as well as the development of humor in learners.

At different ages and levels of cognitive development, learners show distinct preferences for certain types of humor. In the early grades (K–3) children enjoy conceptual incongruity (Burt and Sugawara, 1988) ("It's raining meatballs") and the simple absurdities of riddles, knock-knock jokes, and puns ("It's raining cats and dogs," "I know, I just stepped in a poodle!"). Older elementary (grades 4–6) children find physical humor funny and will frequently laugh when a classmate or an adult experiences physical discomfiture. By middle/junior high school (grades 7–9), humor frequently exhibits cruelty toward peers, diminution of adult authority, or "dirty" jokes. By high school, students' sense of humor becomes more sophisticated and usually correlates with what the teacher finds funny. In citing Gessell, Ilg, and Ames, Nikki Barnhart (1989) summarizes this developmental scheme nicely:

> Pure nonsense is enjoyed at an early stage of humor development, but children between the ages of six and eight would rather participate in humor that is understandable to them. By second grade children can create humor by word play, and some link has been found between cognitive maturity and the comprehension of riddles. Eight-year-olds have a strong humor sense and particularly enjoy stories where one person is fooled by another. By the age of ten, children enjoy slapstick humor as well as practical jokes, puns, and riddles. Twelve-year-olds like practical jokes and teasing as well as corny and smutty jokes. By thirteen, sarcasm begins and in another year humor is used against parents and authority figures. At fifteen, children begin to be able to laugh at themselves and then participate in adult-type humor at sixteen.

Reinforcing this description, McGhee (1971) described the results of studies done in the 1930s and 1940s with students in grades 2 through 12. These studies found that students in grades 7, 9, and 12 expressed preference (most to least) for absurdity, slapstick, satire, and whimsy. Further, children aged 7 to 12 found visual humor most preferable, with little or no appreciation of verbal wit. Children aged 11 to 13 thought that situations involving someone's discomfiture were funniest, whereas 14- to 18-year-olds were characterized by noticeable individual differences in sense of humor, greater appreciation of verbal wit, and reliance on what in a particular situation was funny (McGhee, 1971). Although students today are more sophisticated in their humor and are exposed to a wider variety of humor at an earlier age, the predominant characteristics of humor at each stage are remarkably similar between today's students and their counterparts sixty or seventy years ago.

In general, researchers support the use of humor in the classroom (Rareshide, 1993), although most recommend it be used judiciously (Steele, 1998) and with a clear understanding of the strengths and weaknesses of using humor in any grade level or content area (Dickmeyer, 1993). Some researchers suggest that there is an important link between humor in the classroom and the kind of social climate the teacher establishes in the classroom (Gurtler, 2002). This perspective supports the notion that a teacher can enhance the social climate in the classroom through the incorporation of different types of humor-building strategies or techniques. This, in turn, can help improve the relationship between the teacher and the students and among the students themselves.

Although there are individual differences in preferences for various types of humor, most learners perceive a sense of humor to be essential to effective teaching (Korobkin, 1988). However, what constitutes a sense of humor varies widely, depending on the gender of the teacher, the age and developmental level of the learners, the subject being taught, the particular characteristics of the classroom situation, and of course the personality of the teacher. Some teachers use humor with extraordinary effectiveness, whereas others are ill served by their awkward attempts to make students laugh.

Much of your development as a teacher will involve self-discovery and the ability to identify your strengths and weaknesses in working with learners. You may find that the jokes, stories, quips, and puns that your friends and family laugh at until they cry fall flat when you try them on students. Conversely, you may find the humor that causes your students to collapse into paroxysms of laughter is incredibly unsophisticated or just plain silly. It is unlikely that you will walk into a classroom and become an immediate comedic hit with your first lesson. Indeed, it would be unwise for you to try. Rather, you should be concerned with becoming an observer of humor and a discriminating analyst of humorous situations. You should know when humor is appropriate and when it is distracting, embarrassing, or offensive. You should identify when learning can be enhanced through the use of relevant, insightful forms of humor. Finally, you should be aware that students don't expect their teachers to be stand-up comedians, nor do they perceive it as particularly attractive when their teachers try to be funny in a situation that doesn't call for it.

CLASSIFYING HUMOR IN THE CLASSROOM

In 1991 James Neulip employed an inductive approach to analyze and categorize high school teachers' use of humor in their teaching. Working from a series of studies (Gorham and Christophel, 1990; Nussbaum, Comadena, and Holladay, 1985; Bryant, Comisky, and Zillmann, 1979) done with college students, Neulip expanded upon what he considered to be the limitations of those studies to create a taxonomic approach for classifying high school teachers' humor. This taxonomy contained twenty items organized into five categories: (1) teacher-targeted humor, (2) student-targeted humor, (3) untargeted humor, (4) external source humor, and (5) nonverbal humor (Neulip, 1991).

Teacher-targeted humor involves personal anecdotes disclosed by the teacher that are either related or unrelated to the content or involve some personally embarrassing incident. Other types of teacher-targeted humor utilize role-playing by the teacher that is related to course content (e.g., the teacher becomes Pythagoras while explaining the Pythagorean Theorem) or unrelated to course content (e.g., the teacher mimics the voice of Arnold Schwarzenegger saying "I'll be baack" when leaving the classroom). Finally, another example would be the teacher making a self-deprecating remark (e.g., pointing out his or her own girth when teaching about proper diet).

Student-targeted humor is somewhat trickier to employ because of potential embarrassment and/or uneasiness on the part of the students. Examples of this type of humor include joking good-naturedly about a student's erroneous response or comment, insulting students in a friendly, nonhostile way (e.g., "This group enters the room like a herd of turtles"), teasing students in a nonconfrontational way (e.g., referring to a junior high clique as the "South Park" group because of the clique's emulation of the cast of that show), and student role-playing.

Teachers need to be cautious when using student-targeted humor if it could result in a student becoming the unwitting (and unwilling) recipient of a teacher's use of sarcasm. For example, a student who comes to class with a new nose or eyebrow piercing might be kidded by a teacher who points it out by saying, "Oooh, what a cute nose (or eyebrow) ring. I'm sure your first boss will just love it!" Although the teacher may have a valid point regarding the appropriateness of facial piercings in the workplace, that point should be made privately or as part of a more general discussion about how to dress for a job interview. Singling out a student with such a comment could lead to more aggressive comments by peers and might even be seen as a type of bullying on the part of the teacher. Student-targeted humor should be used judiciously and be well thought out before the comment is made. Spur-of-the-moment attempts at sarcasm are rarely effective as a form of student-targeted humor.

The third category is referred to as *untargeted humor* or, as Neulip points out, issue- or topic-oriented humor. This includes joke telling, punning, tongue-in-cheek statements, and awkward comparisons or incongruity (e.g., using a *Dilbert* cartoon to illustrate how a boss shouldn't act toward employees).

External sources of humor are the fourth category of the taxonomy. These include historical incidents with some humorous slant (e.g., the little girl who suggested that Abraham Lincoln grow a beard), third-party humor that is either related or unrelated to the content (e.g., cartoons, photographs, funny headlines), and natural phenomena (e.g., illustrating how creating a vacuum can suck a hard-boiled egg into a narrow-necked bottle).

Finally, a teacher's use of *nonverbal humor* is the fifth category. This type of humor can be described as being done for affect display (e.g., making a face to show feigned anger) or as part of physical humor to gain student attention through exaggerated gestures or body movements.

Categories like these can help identify the types of humor that teachers employ in the classroom. Although the categorization scheme was designed primarily for use with high school teachers, it can be applied to elementary classrooms. The main difference in humor use between the two settings may be degree rather than kind. We would expect fewer and less sophisticated examples of the types of humor described here, but we would still expect to find aspects of incongruity, joke telling (riddles), physical humor, role-playing (pretend play), teasing, and so forth in the average elementary classroom.

During your observations in elementary, middle/junior high, and high school classrooms, you should become more adept at spotting humorous events, activities, statements, and so forth and determining whether the use of humor was appropriate to the situation. The following Core Activity will give you an instrument that you can use to identify the type, frequency, and appropriateness of humor in the classroom(s) that you're observing.

Core Activity

TEACHER HUMOR CHART

Use the following chart to categorize humorous incidents, activities, events, and so forth during your observations in an elementary or secondary classroom. Use one chart for each classroom that you observe (make copies of the chart if you observe more than one classroom) and indicate the observation dates. Note why you felt a particular example of a teacher's use of humor was either appropriate or inappropriate.

Grade Level: _____ Dates of Observations: _____

Subject(s) Observed: _____

Teacher Gender: _____ Estimated Age of Teacher: _____

TEACHER-TARGETED HUMOR

CATEGORY	APPROPRIATE	INAPPROPRIATE
Self-disclosure related to content:		
Self-disclosure unrelated to content:		
Self-disclosure embarrassment:		
Teacher role-play related to content:		
Teacher role-play unrelated to content:		
Teacher self-deprecation:		

STUDENT-TARGETED HUMOR

CATEGORY	APPROPRIATE	INAPPROPRIATE
Error identification:		
Friendly insult:		
Teasing:		
Student role-play:		

UNTARGETED HUMOR

CATEGORY	APPROPRIATE	INAPPROPRIATE
Awkward comparison/ incongruity:		
Joke telling:		

Punning:

_____

Tongue-in-cheek/
facetious:

_____

EXTERNAL SOURCE HUMOR

CATEGORY	APPROPRIATE	INAPPROPRIATE

Historical incidents:

_____

Third-party humor
related to content
(e.g., cartoons):

_____

Third-party humor
unrelated to content:

_____

Natural phenomena
humor:

_____

NONVERBAL HUMOR

CATEGORY	APPROPRIATE	INAPPROPRIATE

Affect display humor
(e.g., exaggerated
gestures or facial
reaction):

_____

Physical humor:

_____

Category of humor used most frequently: _____

Category of humor used least frequently: _____

Number of appropriate uses of humor: _____

Number of inappropriate uses of humor: _____

Throughout your experience in schools as a learner you probably encountered a number of teachers who used, or attempted to use, humor in their teaching. However, you may have had other memorable humorous experiences in school that occurred outside the classroom. By and large, most critics of schools depict them as repressive, humorless places where few, if any, fun activities occur. Indeed, it often appears to such critics that teachers and school administrators consciously try to squelch humor in any form, whether teacher-targeted, student-targeted, or student-generated. In the following Suggested Activity you are asked to recall a humorous person, incident, or event that you found memorable. Try to identify the characteristics that made this person, incident, or event particularly funny and, if possible, relate the humor to the categorization scheme described earlier in this chapter.

Suggested Activity

FUNNY INCIDENTS IN SCHOOL

Describe the following in as much detail as possible:

1. The funniest person you knew in school:

_____

_____

_____

_____

_____

_____

_____

2. The funniest teacher you knew in school:

_____

_____

_____

_____

_____

_____

_____

3. The most humorous situation that you recall happening at school for which no one got into trouble:

_____

_____

_____

_____

_____

_____

4. The most humorous situation that you recall happening at school for which one or more persons got into trouble:

_____

_____

_____

_____

_____

_____

5. The most memorable situation in school in which the use of humor went wrong. Who attempted it and why was the result disastrous?

_____

_____

_____

_____

_____

Student Name: _____ Date: _____

Journal Entry

During this chapter you were asked to identify and categorize behaviors of teachers that were intended to be humorous. You were also asked to judge the appropriateness of the use of humor in the classroom. In this Journal Entry, try to analyze your own sense of humor and predict whether humor will likely be an element in your teaching style. In addition, suggest ways in which classrooms and schools might become places where humor is appreciated and utilized more effectively and frequently.

_____
_____
_____
_____
_____
_____
_____
_____
_____
_____
_____
_____
_____
_____

Questions for Discussion

1. Based on your observations, which types of humor were employed most frequently by elementary teachers? By secondary teachers? How do these totals compare with your expectations? In what ways could the teachers have employed humor more frequently? Less frequently?

2. To what extent was the use of humor appropriate to the situation, age of the students, subject/topic being taught, and personality of the teacher? What would you have done differently?

3. Some research studies have suggested that males use humor more frequently and more effectively than females and that students respond better to male teachers' humor. More recent studies, however, dispute this. What did you find in your observations when you compared them with your classmates'? Were there observable gender differences in terms of effective use of humor?

4. What differences in type, frequency, and appropriateness of humor did you find in classrooms of teachers who were under 30 years of age? Ages 31 to 45? Ages 46 to 60? Over 60? Is teacher age an important factor to consider when studying humor in the classroom?

References

Barnhart, N. C. (1989, Winter). Humor: An art in itself. *Delta Kappa Gamma Bulletin, 55,* 9–12.

Bryant, J., Comisky, P., and Zillmann, D. (1979). Teachers' humor in the college classroom. *Communication Education, 28,* 110–118.

Burt, L. M., and Sugawara, A. I. (1988). Children's humor and implications for teaching. *Early Childhood Development Care, 37,* 13–25.

Costa, A. L., and Kallick, B. (Eds.). (2000). *Discovering and exploring habits of mind.* Alexandria, VA: Association for Supervision and Curriculum Development.

Dickmeyer, S. (1993, April). *Humor as an instructional practice: A longitudinal content analysis of humor use in the classroom.* Paper presented at the annual meeting of the Eastern Communication Association, New Haven, CT, April 28–May 2, 1993. EDRS Document: ED 359 587.

Gorham, J., and Christophel, D. M. (1990, January). The relationship of teachers' use of humor in the classroom to immediacy and student learning. *Communication Education, 39,* 40–62.

Gurtler, Leo. (2002, August). *Humor in educational contexts.* Paper presented at the annual meeting of the American Psychological Association, Chicago, IL, August 22–25, 2002. EDRS Document: ED 470 407.

Korobkin, D. (1988, Fall). Humor in the classroom: Considerations and strategies. *College Teaching, 36,* 154–158.

McGhee, P. (1971). Development of the humor response: A review of literature. *Psychological Bulletin, 76,* 328–348.

Neulip, J. W. (1991, October). An examination of the content of high school teachers' humor in the classroom and the development of an inductively derived taxonomy of classroom humor. *Communication Education, 40,* 343–355.

Nussbaum, J. F., Comadena, M. E., and Holladay, S. J. (1985, May). *Verbal communication within the college classroom.* Paper presented at the meeting of the International Communication Association, Chicago, IL.

Rareshide, Stephen W. (1993). *Implications for teachers' use of humor in the classroom.* Research Report. EDRS Document: ED 359 165.

Steele, Karen. (1998). *The positive and negative effects of the use of humor in the classroom setting.* Unpublished master's thesis. Salem-Tiekyo University. EDRS Document: ED 426 929.

Vance, C. M. (1987). Comparative study on humor and design of instruction. *Instructional Science, 16(1),* 79–100.

Ziv, A. (Fall 1988). Teaching and learning with humor: Experiment and replication. *Journal of Experimental Education, 57,* 5–15.

Chapter 9

THE TEACHER AND ETHICS

When we visit a school, or simply reflect on our own experiences in school, we see people and buildings, books and charts, desks and chalkboards. All of these pieces are part of the intellectual mission of schools: to pass on to the next generation the knowledge that the older generation is convinced that the next generation will need to survive and to prosper. The observer can "see" this mission in action as teachers explain or drill and as students read or compute. The rituals and routines of school, from "paying attention" to taking tests, are oriented to this very apparent and obvious knowledge goal of schools.

Another mission of schools, although less obvious, is equally important. It goes by many names: "character education," "moral education," "education for citizenship," and "the teaching of values." Essentially, though, the mission is to ensure that young people acquire the ethical standards and enduring moral habits they will need to manage their own lives and to contribute to the common good.

This moral mission of schools is not new. It is no fad. It reaches the core of what it is to be educated, to be a person. Socrates said that the task of education is to make a person both smart and good. Many philosophers and thinkers have seen this ethical goal of education as even more fundamental than education's intellectual goal. Likewise, many parents are more concerned that their children are good than that they are smart. They want their children to grow up to be people with a clear sense of right and wrong, people who can be relied upon to do their share, to be loyal to their families and their nation, and to be honest in their dealings with others. Academic success is important to them, but it is not in the same league as raising "good children."

Fortunately, however, these two goals are not in conflict. It is not a matter of "either/or." Schools and teachers can and should help children develop both knowledge (content and intellectual skills) and ethical values and positive character traits. In fact, these two goals should go hand in hand.

Some people who are considering careers in education may be uneasy with the idea of schools and teachers being involved in the moral education of the young. They wonder exactly whose values should be taught, a question of particular concern to ethnic and religious minorities. In a highly pluralistic nation like the United States, it is important for public schools not to violate the ethical views of individual groups. Nor should our tax-supported schools undermine the positive values taught in homes. But although teachers should be vigilant against that possibility, there are some strong arguments for teachers' active involvement in character formation and the acquisition of moral values. Among these are the following:

- Great philosophers and thinkers from ancient times (Socrates, Plato, and Aristotle) to the modern era (John Dewey to John Goodlad) have taught that moral values and character development are a major part of education. Drawing on the Greek philosopher Aristotle, Jon Moline (1981) has written, "People do not naturally or spontaneously grow up to be morally excellent or practically wise. They become so, if at all, only as the result of a lifetime of personal and community effort."

- Our nation's founders (Washington, Jefferson, Franklin, and Madison) were anxious to create an education system that would teach and develop the moral values, such as respect for the rights of others, personal responsibility, and tolerance, that are the foundation stones of a democratic society.

- The codes of education in most states explicitly point out that it is not simply the right of teachers, but their responsibility, to teach values and moral habits that are fundamental to good citizenship. In addition, the legislatures in state after state in recent years have reaffirmed the need for schools to be more active and effective in this area.

- For almost twenty-five years public opinion polls have demonstrated that four out of five Americans want public schools to take an active role in the moral education and character formation of the young. This percentage is higher among respondents who have children in public schools. When people are asked whether schools should teach core American moral values such as honesty, responsibility, and justice, the positive responses are in the 90–100 percent range.

- Finally, a negative supporting point: It is impossible to teach school *without* affecting a child's sense of right and wrong, how they should behave and not behave, and other morally related issues. By their nature, schools are moral institutions with people continually behaving in good and bad ways. The curriculum is filled with stories of good and bad deeds. Given the inevitability of the moral nature of schools, it seems best to address this issue and deal with it openly.

It would appear, then, that there is a strong case for the public schools taking an active and positive role in the moral education and character formation of students. Still, however, many educators are confused about how to proceed.

WHAT "PRODUCT" SHOULD THE PUBLIC SCHOOLS SEEK?

An old adage says that you can't get where you are going if you don't know where it is. This holds true, in general, for education and, in particular, for the moral and ethical goals of schooling. One way for teachers to conceive of this is to aim at developing a morally mature person. Working with a child's family, church, and community, educators see themselves contributing to the making of a person, to a "final product" who can think, feel, and act in a morally mature way. Said another way, the teacher should help students to know the good, love the good, and do the good.

KNOWING THE GOOD

Every community has a view of "the good life." Usually unstated, this is a vision of how people ought to live to be personally happy and to be contributing members of society. It is a fundamental task of schools to help children come to know that vision of the good life and how to attain it. Anthropologists and social psychologists, who study how people live together in groups, might describe this effort as the adults of a community socializing the young into the morality of the tribe. Without this shared vision of what is right and what is wrong, a society would begin to fall apart. This shared vision can also be called *moral literacy*. Morally literate people know, for instance, that they ought to

- Be honest in their dealings with others.
- Respect the rights of others.
- Behave responsibly in their work and to those around them.
- Be concerned with the underdogs and those less fortunate than they are.

Morally literate people know these social *shoulds* and how they contribute to a better life.

True teachers are not interested in developing children into simple "rule keepers." Therefore, it is important that students know how to think through moral and ethical issues. They must be able to consider questions such as "What is the right thing to do in this situation?" and "What are the consequences of this or that course of action?" As citizens, graduates of our schools must be able to fulfill the requirements of democratic citizenship. They must be able to select the most ethical solutions to civic problems, solutions that both protect the individual and serve the common good. Teachers, then, need to know that part of their job is to teach students these core human values.

LOVING THE GOOD

Life is not all "sweet reason." When we make moral decisions and ethical choices, our emotions and desires have a strong influence on us. The heart is a crucial element in moral education. If a child is totally in love with himself—that is, if he is truly "selfish"—he is a danger to himself and those around him. One important function of school, therefore, is to help children love the right things—the right people, the right ideas, and the right actions.

As teachers, we must touch the heart. Warren Nord has stated it nicely: "The relationship between feeling and reason in ethics is complex and controversial, but certainly morality is grounded to some considerable extent in the moral feelings—compassion, guilt, hope, despair, dignity, mercy, and love, for example. When ethics is stripped of its emotional dimensions, it becomes artificial, abstract, and lifeless." It is the work of education to help students love the right things and especially the right image of what kinds of people they hope to become.

DOING THE GOOD

Knowing the good and loving the good are important, but behavior is the bottom line. Behavior is, as the old expression goes, where the rubber meets the road. What we actually do is the true standard of moral persons. Many of us can intellectually come up with the morally right course of action and even want to do the right thing, but doing what is right is the real test. For instance, on the school bus, when other children are making life miserable for another child, a particular student may know what the right thing to do is and may even want to stop the teasing and meanness, but she may simply let it all happen.

Implicit in this expectation that the school help children do the good is the need for teachers to help children practice moral action. Teachers must set up opportunities for students to "do the good." They must help students engage in moral action and help them acquire the enduring habits that make good character. They must give them opportunities to practice the "good life" that they come to know through stories and instruction. They must help students not simply to know how important it is for citizens to be responsible, but also to behave responsibly.

Helping the student become a morally mature person is a slow process. It is also quite different from first grade to middle school to high school. To ignore this domain, however, is impossible. As we have stated, the school cannot host children from the time they are 5 until 17 or 18 and not profoundly affect how they think and feel about issues of right and wrong and how they act. School, with all its rewards and punishments and social tugging and towing, cannot help but have a strong moral impact on students. Like it or not, moral education and the teaching of good character—for good or ill—are inevitable parts of school.

WHAT CAN SCHOOLS AND TEACHERS DO?

School is a swirling cauldron of moral matter: students bullying one another, teachers gossiping, students volunteering to help a classmate, teachers staying after school to work with a child returning after an illness, teachers playing favorites, students writing graffiti in the lavatories, and so on. Inevitably the school sends powerful moral messages to the student. The matter, however, should not be left to chance. The classroom and the school can positively affect the moral maturity of the student in specific ways. What follows are the authors' "five *E*s of moral and character education"—*example*, *explanation*, *exhortation*, *ethos*, and *experience*.

EXAMPLE

Although the expectation that we as teachers must be "good examples" to our students may be unsettling to many of us (even paralyzing us with fear), there is really no way around this fact. Students spend long hours during the all-important formative period of their lives in close observation of teachers. The unseen but ever-present "project" of a child is to become a successful adult.

Anyone who has ever had children in school or who has listened to students talk about their teachers knows that students only occasionally concern themselves with their teachers' instructional strategies or skills. Whether the teacher uses audiovisual materials well or can use a variety of questioning techniques is rarely commented on. Students do, however, complain about and praise the teacher's moral qualities. "She is so unfair!" "Last year my teacher played favorites, but Miss Kinsella treats everyone the same." "At the beginning of the year Mr. Oliver said that he would stay after school and help anyone having difficulties, and he really means it." "Anyone can see that Mrs. Doyle loves the smart kids and hates the rest of us!"

A few years ago a cartoon in *The New Yorker* magazine depicted a fifth-grade student telling her stunned father, "What did we learn in school today? Well, we learned that Paris is cool. Amsterdam is groovy. And Miss Fisher isn't going to marry that guy in the black leather jacket who picks her up every day after school with his motorcycle." Although Miss Fisher's lesson plan may have said that the day's educational goals were to teach long division and how deserts are formed, the enduring lessons may have been quite different.

The great English parliamentarian and social philosopher Edmund Burke once wrote, "Example is the school of mankind, and they will learn at no other." Teachers are de facto moral exemplars or models in numerous ways, from our thoughtfulness to those around us to how we react to students' cheating. Perhaps the most powerful way in which we teach moral values is least discussed: the way we do our work.

Whether surgeons or shoemakers or second-grade teachers, people have a moral responsibility to be excellent at their craft. Although the surgeon's work is hidden and the shoemaker's seams unseen, the teacher's craft is continually on display. We are role models, which doesn't mean just passively standing around and being looked at! We model by what we do and how we do it—specifically by

- The way that we prepare our lessons and classes.
- The promptness and thoroughness with which we correct papers and exams.
- The care that we take to see that students are actually learning.
- Our lack of tolerance for wasting time.
- The accuracy of our grades and records.
- The effort that we give to those who need more advanced work and those who need special help.
- The standards that we set for ourselves and our students.
- Being learners and keeping up with our field.

Another way that teachers impart good values and important character traits is through the curriculum. One way to view the school's curriculum is as society's choice of what is most worth knowing. Prominent among this mass of ideas, skills, and information are the individual people who have contributed to our progress and success and those who have betrayed their responsibilities to those around them. So history and biography are important components of schooling. Our children must know from our own national heritage Thomas Jefferson, Benedict Arnold, Abraham Lincoln, Harriet Tubman, Andrew Carnegie, Jane Addams, Huey Long, and Franklin and Eleanor Roosevelt. They must know, too, the moral examples in our literature because these characters are frequently the embodiment of our ethical ideals. They learn courage from *The Scarlet Letter*'s Hester Prynne and the price of hypocrisy from the book's Arthur Dimmesdale. From Huck Finn's struggle with his conscience over whether to turn in the runaway slave Jim, students learn that established laws and public views are not always correct. From *To Kill a Mockingbird*'s Atticus Finch they learn how a morally mature individual meets his responsibilities to his family, his neighbors, and his community. Although this moral dimension of literature often receives scant attention in our classrooms, it is a powerful conveyor of our society's moral exemplars and ideals.

EXPLANATION

Knowing the good means that we understand what is right and correct. A child needs to learn that punching someone who frustrates him is not a good way to behave. She needs to learn why she cannot spread lies about another student or cheat on an examination. Through fear and punishment, students can be trained to behave. However, unless they understand why standards exist, once they are out of school, their behavior may revert to settling matters by antisocial methods.

Knowing the good means that we can think through issues of right and wrong and come up with ethical decisions. This intellectual skill does not just happen. Much of what a teacher does is explaining. We explain cause and effect. We explain the need to get the facts. We explain how to draw correct conclusions. We explain our society's rules and why and how we look out for the underdog. And we explain why and how we follow our Constitution. We correct faulty ethical reasoning ("I hit him because he gave me a mean look"). Critical thinking or reasoning skills have a great deal to do with citizenship and our moral lives. The work of the teacher, then, involves explaining not only the content of our social rules, but also the process. Students need to be able to think through the ethical issues that inevitably will face them as adults and as citizens.

EXHORTATION

The *exhortation* that we write of is an exhortation to the heart. As suggested earlier, there are times when sweet reason fails. The children on the bus continue to pick on one lonely child. They understand why it is not a good thing to make the child so unhappy. Each knows that he or she should buck the crowd and "do the right thing." But they do not. Then there are students who confront terrible problems from physical handicaps to divorcing parents. They are depressed and discouraged. Like the children on the bus, they can see no reason to change their attitude. It is here that the teacher needs to make an appeal to the heart, to that image that each child has of the good person each wants to be. Whether it is a pep talk or a stern reminder, the teacher employs emotions to appeal to students' moral emotions. And although this exhortation should never be far from rational explanation, it is essentially an appeal to the heart.

An important foundation for these appeals to the heart is helping children develop an image of the good person—the ideal self that can be appealed to. This is another reason for children to have storehouses of "good examples" or personal heroes in their minds. To the degree that our heroes and heroines are understood and admired, they exert a positive pull on us.

Another aspect of this appeal to the heart is the ability to empathize. Morally mature individuals are able "to walk in the shoes of the people they meet." They feel the suffering of others and the injustice that others are experiencing. They can put themselves into the place of the child who is being mistreated by bus mates. They can understand what it feels like to be a slave. There is something inside these students to which the teacher can direct his or her exhortations.

ETHOS

Ethos is a word of Greek origin that refers to the character or the distinguishing attitudes and habits of a place or a person. Like a sorority house, a boot camp, or a prison, a school has an ethos. This ethos is unseen, but it is also a powerful influence on those present. The ethos of a place says what kind of behavior is encouraged or tolerated. It speaks to the standards of the place, the qualities of the human relations among people, and what is rewarded and what is punished. (Another "*E*" word is *environment*, as in "the moral environment of the place.")

Most experienced educators can enter a school building, whether elementary or secondary, urban or suburban, public or private, and rather quickly get a sense of the moral ethos. The moral climate can be sensed in how people address one another. Sullen students, aloof teachers, and hostile staff reflect one kind of ethos. Engaged students, involved teachers, and courteous staff are strong indicators of attitudes and personal habits that are part of a positive moral ethos. In recent years much has been written about the "hidden curriculum" of the school: all of the learning that is not written in the formal documents of the school but still gets taught in school—such as not telling the teacher what you *really* thought of the first act of *King Lear* or how to avoid gym on days when you are feeling awful. This true learning is part of the hidden curriculum. But so, too, are the attitudes and moral standards that we absorb from the moral climate of the school.

Although a school's "ethos" sounds like a vague abstraction that would be out of the control of an educator, just the opposite is true. Some classroom teachers have made their rooms a safe haven and a productive work scene in schools that are otherwise chaotic. In other classrooms students have become hostile and aggressive in schools that are otherwise cooperative and relaxed. The point is that the classroom ethos or school ethos is made. It is a place where there are fair rules, evenly enforced. It is a place where there is an air of responsibility that is shared by all. Typically ethos is the product of the professional staff working together to create a certain kind of climate. But whether or not a school has a morally positive ethos, we can be sure of one thing: Ethos teaches.

EXPERIENCE

We live in a world of images and symbols. For many children, television is the primary window onto reality. We also live in a world where there are limited out-of-school opportunities to work. Modern life seems to have conspired to keep many children from real encounters with life, ones that make serious demands on them and from which they can grow into confident adults. In an earlier era, the young man learning farming at his father's side and the older sister living in a large family had demands thrust upon them. And although many changes in modern life have been positive, modern life has robbed our young of many of the maturing experiences of the past. James Coleman, a distinguished sociologist, has stated, "American youth are information rich and experience poor." It is impossible to become a fully developed adult without maturing experiences.

A primary task of schools is to work with family and community to help children become contributing members of society. "Contributing members" means people who look out for others, who think of themselves as helpers, and who have the skills needed to help others. School is an ideal place for children to learn both that they ought to be helpers and how to be helpers. Although learning that they *ought* to contribute to others and the common good was discussed earlier, *learning* is our subject here.

Children learn how to be helpers by structured activities such as these:

- A carefully monitored cooperative activity in which they are shown how to be of direct aid to one another.
- Having a specific task to perform regularly that benefits the class or the school (feeding the gerbil and cleaning its cage or picking up trash in a certain area of the school).

- Volunteering to help the teacher or librarian as an aide, doing clerical or routine tasks.
- Being part of a class that once a month helps out an elderly couple having trouble keeping up with their house.
- Taking on a community service project, such as spending an afternoon each week reading to the blind.

Students can learn the skills of being a contributor through unstructured experiences like these:

- Helping another student who is having difficulty with an assignment.
- Befriending a new or lonely student.
- Being a peacemaker between warring friends or groups.
- Standing up against injustice, such as playground bullying or students unfairly spreading rumors about another student.

Although knowing the good and loving the good are important, doing the good is, in effect, life's bottom line. Moral actors are not only what we should be aiming for in school, but they are also the means. The philosopher Aristotle claimed that a person becomes virtuous (that is, a person of good habits) by doing good things. We become brave by doing brave acts. We become kind by doing kind acts. Teachers, then, must make sure that there are opportunities, structured and unstructured, for students to become moral actors.

Although values and character cannot be seen, the classroom or school that is attending to its moral mission has certain observable qualities. These qualities are our five *E*s of moral and character education.

The teacher, by definition, is involved with a deeply ethical enterprise. Henry Adams wrote, "A teacher affects eternity: No one can tell where his influence stops." The work of the teacher involves subject matter and instructional technique, but all of this is permeated by the ethical. We find ourselves asking questions like these:

- What are the important moral ideas in this story or in this historical event?
- What are the reasons why I insist that children respect one another and not fight or use crude language?
- Why don't I allow cheating, and why do I insist on honesty?
- Why am I so concerned that my top students are so terribly competitive?
- What can I do to help make George less selfish?

In all of these questions we are recognizing the intricate moral nature of classrooms. But unlike the intellectual nature and the knowledge mission, it is woven into the very fabric of schooling. For this reason it is important that the future teacher look at schools and classrooms through the lens of the school's ethical and character-forming missions.

Suggested Activity 1

INTERVIEWING ON THE MORAL DOMAIN

Try to have a private conversation with the teacher whom you have been observing, or a teacher of your acquaintance, about his or her perception of the teacher's role as a model educator. Generate a list of your own questions, but consider using some of these:

1. Do you consciously try to teach and promote certain moral values in your classroom? Which ones? How do you do this?

2. Are there moral values that you would like to teach but that you think are inappropriate for public schools? Why?

3. What good habits are you trying to promote in your classroom?

4. Have you ever received support or encouragement from parents for stressing moral values and issues of character? Have you ever encountered problems or objections?

5. What is a serious ethical issue you have confronted in the classroom? In this school?

6. Do other teachers in this school discuss the ethical and moral aspects of their work with children? Do you feel encouragement or support from your administrators?

Provide your own questions about moral and character education here:

_____

_____

_____

_____

_____

_____

_____

_____

_____

_____

Amanda Gordon is a first-year teacher nearing the home stretch. She has been teaching social studies in a rural middle school since early August. Now, close to ten months later, she can almost see the finish line. It has been a roller coaster of a year with enough highs and lows for a lifetime. Reflecting on the year now, as she monitors her after-lunch class's final exam, Amanda has a good feeling about the year. Yes, she made her share of rookie mistakes, some of which almost cause her to blush. And, yes, there were mornings she dreaded coming to school. But there were incredible highs, too. She did things with her class that she never thought she was capable of. The absolute "high of highs," however, was when one of the senior teachers told her that her no-nonsense principal had remarked, "That Gordon kid really seems to have the right stuff." Okay, she didn't like the "kid" part, but the rest was terrific. And shortly after that she received the much anticipated invitation and contract to return next year.

In the midst of her reverie, Amanda noticed a student clearly copying answers from another student's answer sheet. She casually moved to the back of the room to get a better view of what was going on. Not to her surprise, the cheater was Floyd Taylor, the student with whom she had had the most difficulty this year. "Difficult" doesn't quite capture the pain and anxiety Floyd had caused her. Floyd was a mouthy, lazy, sneaky bully. Right now he had poor Richie Altman's answer sheet on his desk. And this was the sneaky and bullying Floyd at work. Floyd knew that Richie was not only one of the best students in the class, but the one whom he could bully without fear of consequences.

Amanda decided not to make a scene; but after collecting the papers, she would detain both of them, march them to the principal's office, and lay the matter before him. Talk about "red-handed!" She had Floyd cold. He would never wriggle his way out of this one. Just then she noticed something under Gilda White's test paper. Gilda was her "star," probably her favorite student, and she wondered what it was. Coming up behind Gilda's desk, she realized that whatever it was had writing on it. When Gilda sensed she was near, she tried to hide whatever it was. Amanda quietly reached under Gilda's answer sheet, retrieved the paper, and returned to the back of the room. When she looked at the paper, she knew immediately that it was a cheat sheet of course notes. In a very fine hand Gilda had written an outline of the course's most important information. Amanda was dumbfounded. Gilda was the last student in her class that she would have predicted would cheat. Then Amanda remembered hearing that Gilda's parents put an enormous amount of pressure on their daughter. Amanda had realized, too, during the year that although Gilda was a "star," she had to work extremely hard to keep up with the other class leaders. But how could Gilda have done this? Then Amanda realized she had to act. Turning Gilda in for cheating would destroy her. She was already a driven, rather anxious girl. And how would her parents react? Right now no one but Gilda knew that Amanda had taken the notes. Should she . . . could she turn Gilda in? Should she give Gilda a good talking to and maybe give her a new exam? But if she did that for Gilda, what about Floyd? What was the right thing to do? What was the fair thing to do? The exam was almost over, and Amanda knew she had to act!

DISCUSSION

Spend a few minutes reviewing the facts of this case. Then jot down exactly what you would do. Remember: "Not to decide is to decide." Now answer these questions:

1. What actions should Amanda have taken? For what reasons?
2. What are the best reasons for not taking the action you are suggesting?
3. Do you think it is possible for a teacher not to have favorites? Do you think it is positive not to "play" favorites?
4. If you would treat the two cheating cases differently, what are the bases for your actions?
5. Can you remember other such moral conflicts confronted by your teachers?

Core Activity
STUDENT OBSERVATION ACTIVITY

Over a period of thirty minutes, focus exclusively on the moral dimension of a student's experience. In the space that follows, jot down observational notes about the influences on and activities affecting the student. Try to keep your notes descriptive and nonjudgmental. To help you sort out the experience, we suggest that you organize your notes under the headings of the five *E*s described earlier.

1. *Examples:*
   Teacher:

   _____

   _____

   _____

   _____

   _____

   _____

   Other students:

   _____

   _____

   _____

   _____

   _____

   _____

People in the curriculum (in stories or in discussions of current events):

_____

_____

_____

_____

_____

_____

Other examples (pictures of famous people on the walls):

_____

_____

_____

_____

_____

_____

2. *Explanations:*
   Teacher talk about rules or discipline or ethical issues:

_____

_____

_____

_____

_____

_____

Student talk about rules or other ethical issues:

_____

_____

_____

_____

_____

_____

Direct teaching about what is the correct thing to do:

_____

_____

_____

_____

_____

_____

3. *Exhortations:*
   Direct appeals by teachers to do the right thing (or to "desist from doing the wrong thing"):

_____

_____

_____

_____

_____

_____

Praise or scolding for certain behaviors:

_____

_____

_____

_____

_____

_____

4. *Ethos:*
   What in the moral climate of this classroom helps or hinders the moral learning of the student?

   _____

   _____

   _____

   _____

   _____

   _____

   What are the signs of a "healthy" or "unhealthy" moral environment?

   _____

   _____

   _____

   _____

   _____

   _____

5. *Experiences:*
   Is there evidence of moral action in this classroom? _____

   Are there opportunities to be helpful? _____

   Are students encouraged to be helpful? _____

   Do they take the opportunities? _____

   Does this class have opportunities for students to practice selfish or mean-spirited activities against one another? _____

6. *Other:*

   _____

   _____

   _____

   _____

   _____

   _____

Based on your school observation, fill in the following checklist of activities and programs that have been associated with a school having a strong moral environment:

1. There is a recognition program for positive conduct (i.e., service to others).

   _____

2. Students and their parents get regular feedback on the moral dimension of their school experience (e.g., marks for conduct).

   _____

3. The halls and classrooms display pictures of cultural heroes and/or inspirational sayings.

   _____

4. The school has a mission statement that includes the moral domain.

   _____

5. There is a written code of conduct for this classroom/school, and the students are well aware of it.

   _____

6. There are effective student organizations that directly promote responsible conduct (e.g., SADD).

   _____

7. There is regular evidence of mutual respect observable in this school.

   _____

Student Name:_____ Date:_____

Journal Entry

In this Journal Entry, focus on schools and classrooms as environments for character and moral education. Pay particular attention to the role that the teacher plays as well as to how moral and ethical issues are integrated into the curriculum.

_____

_____

_____

_____

_____

_____

_____

_____

_____

_____

_____

_____

_____

_____

_____

_____

_____

_____

_____

_____

Questions for Discussion

1. What should be the role of the school in helping students to identify, clarify, or modify their values?

2. How do the moral and character formation needs of children vary from elementary to middle to high school?

3. Are some content areas better suited for presenting students with moral and ethical dilemmas? If so, which ones? Why do you believe that they are better suited for this role?

4. What role does the teacher play in providing a model for students in terms of moral and ethical behavior? Should teachers be hired and tenured on the basis of their ability to provide an appropriate role model for students?

5. Based on your observations, which, if any, of the "five *E*s" of moral and character education currently exist in the schools with which you are most familiar? Which appear to be more powerful? Which need to be incorporated more fully into schools?

6. Are some ethical and moral issues too controversial for teachers to discuss with students? If so, which ones? How did the teachers whom you observed handle controversial issues? Did you agree with them?

Reference

Moline, J. N. (1981). Classical ideas about moral education. *Character 2(8),* 8.

Chapter 10

EMBRACING THE CHALLENGE OF DIVERSITY AND INDIVIDUAL DIFFERENCES IN AMERICAN CLASSROOMS

In twenty-first-century America, when individuals choose teaching as a career, many are making a positive statement about their willingness to embrace the opportunities and challenges associated with student diversity. Today classroom teachers routinely face increased diversity in students' ethnicity, linguistic and cultural backgrounds, family structures, socioeconomic status, intellectual aptitude, technological resources, learning styles, and types of learning disability or challenge. As the Davidmans note (2001, p. xi), "More diversity and complexity appear to be inevitable as increased numbers of immigrants from around the world seek out their part in the American drama, and teachers work with families and students suffering from severe levels of economic deprivation."

ECONOMICALLY CHALLENGED STUDENTS

Probably the clearest and most unfortunate example of this deprivation is the ongoing presence of homeless students in P–12 classrooms. For example, in 2000 the U.S. Department of Education estimated that out of 930,232 homeless children, 620,764 were enrolled in school with 519,842 attending regularly. Several years later the same department reported that those 930,232 homeless children represented an approximate increase of 10 percent between 1997 and 2000, and two-thirds of those children were between the ages of 5 and 12 (U.S. Interagency Council on Homelessness, 2004, p. 6).

The teaching profession has not ignored this reality. In all fifty states, in more than 1,200 teacher education programs and in approximately 15,000 school districts, educators have accepted, with varying degrees of commitment, the responsibility of educating highly diverse groups and individuals to their fullest potential. This uneven commitment to supporting equity and diversity is part of the tradition, legislative framework, and sometimes merely the symbolic rhetoric of American education within an advanced capitalistic democracy. Symbolic rhetoric notwithstanding, this tradition is what gives the American classroom special standing among the classrooms of the world—at least in the potential that it holds for second language learners, newly arrived immigrants and refugees, and the physically challenged, culturally different, and poverty afflicted. For future teachers it is particularly noteworthy that in 2004 data provided by Columbia University's National Center for Children in Poverty (NCCP) revealed that many American children are growing up in "poor" or "low-income" families. To make sense of the NCCP data, we must first understand how this organization defines poor and low-income families. For the NCCP a poor family is one whose total earnings equal 100 percent or less of the U.S. federal poverty level (FPL), and the earnings of a low-income family are no more than twice the FPL. In 2004 the FPL was $18,850 for a family of four, $15,670 for a family of three, and $12,490 for a family of two, and according to the NCCP ". . . on average, families need an income equal to about two times the FPL to meet their most basic needs" (Douglas-Hall and Koball, 2005). Given these numerical definitions, the following facts will make clear that for American teachers the challenge of diversity will be heavily influenced by students living, as best they can, in America's poverty zones:

1. In 2002, across the United States, approximately 41 percent of young children (children under 6 years of age) lived in low-income families, and these children, like poor children of all ages, tended to live in the southeastern and southwestern states (Douglas-Hall and Koball, 2004).

2. In 2003 there were approximately 70 million children (newborns to 17 years of age) in the United States. Seventeen percent (11 million) of these children lived in poor families, and 21 percent (16 million) lived in low-income families. The combination of poor and low-income families was 38 percent of the total (27 million) (Douglas-Hall and Koball, 2005).

3. In 2002, states in which the rate of children living in low-income families was 39 percent or higher included the following:

Alabama (43%)	Montana (45%)
Arizona (44%)	Nevada (39%)
Arkansas (53%)	New Mexico (51%)
California (42%)	New York (39%)
District of Columbia (49%)	North Carolina (40%)
Florida (41%)	North Dakota (39%)
Georgia (39%)	Oklahoma (48%)
Idaho (41%)	South Carolina (39%)
Kentucky (40%)	Tennessee (41%)
Louisiana (49%)	Texas (46%)
Mississippi (49%)	West Virginia (49%)

Thus in 2002 there were twenty-one such states in addition to the District of Columbia (Douglas-Hall and Koball, 2004).

This statistical story tells us that learning how to reach, teach, and inspire economically challenged students will be a big part of the diversity equation for some time to come.

Such classrooms, filled with new levels of complexity and diversity, have the potential to make teaching a fascinating and emotionally rewarding career. But diversity can cut two ways. It can be challenging and rewarding, but it can also be stressful and overwhelming. Although your teacher education program will gradually give you skills and knowledge to meet the challenge of diversity, your own personality, attitudes, and willingness to develop new skills will play a major role in defining how diversity affects your career. Are you willing, *por ejemplo*, to become a second *lengua* learner yourself at this early stage in your professional development?

THE VOCABULARY OF DIVERSITY

With the importance of modeling in mind, some of this chapter's activities will introduce you to teachers who provide positive examples of successfully embracing the challenge of diversity; other activities will heighten your awareness of specific elements of diversity. However, before describing these activities, we will discuss some of the key terms associated with diversity. Our remarks will prepare you for the variety of definitions that exist, as well as for the activities that follow, and any interviews that you choose to develop related to content in this chapter. The terms that we address are *multicultural education*, *multiethnic education*, *educational equity*, *special education*, *mainstreaming*, *education for the gifted and talented*, *bilingual/bicultural education*, *at-risk learners*, *bullying, learning styles*, and *social construction of knowledge*.

The Social Construction of Knowledge

This is an imposing list of terms, and several of the terms have more than one meaning. With this variety in mind, Figure 10.2 includes a strategy that we call *multiperspective teaching of American, Canadian, Mexican, and world history* (note that we could have substituted other specific nations, such as Japan, Nigeria, and Russia, because multiperspective teaching applies to all nations and all content). Multiperspective teaching is based on two ideas and is related to a third: the *social construction of knowledge*. First, individuals and groups will often have different views about a particular event or explanation because of the culture and era of which they are a part. Second, it is liberating and wise for students to learn history in a manner that consistently exposes them to these various, often competing, perspectives.

As learners study history in this manner they develop an implicit awareness of a key multicultural education concept—the social construction of knowledge. What is left implicit for students needs to be made explicit herc for future teachers. As the Davidmans note,

> The idea that knowledge is a social construction, and more specifically that social and bureaucratic concepts and categories like race, ethnicity, exceptionality, socioeconomic status, gender, and religion are based on subjective criteria invented by human beings, is critically important for teachers and students to comprehend as they develop their moral vision and voice. (2001, p. 4)

As Mary Kay Thompson Tetreault reminds us, all of these terms, indeed "all works in literature, science, and history . . . have an author—male or female, white or ethnic or racial minority, elite or middle-class or occasionally poor—with motivations and beliefs" (1993, p. 130).

We believe that awareness of these observations will prepare future teachers to question the concepts, assumptions, and knowledge claims of various authority figures such as media pundits, political and religious leaders, college professors, and textbook writers. Such questioning is an essential component of the curriculum reform

"Of course it's misspelled. I'm preserving my indigenous cultural dialect."

Holt, Rinehart and Winston

movement known as multicultural education, as well as of the knowledge base and temperament underlying what American colleges call the "liberal arts."

Thus, while we define some basic multicultural terms, we remind you that there are other definitions of these terms—and indeed other critical terms—that we do not share for reasons that we see and don't see (reasons that are linked to our socio-cultural identities). Now, with social construction confessions made, and with humility, let us turn to our definitions.

Multicultural Education

Within the set of terms listed, *multicultural education* has the broadest sweep, and several writers see it as an educational movement that subsumes all the other terms. It is also an emergent concept that has been defined in various ways. Several early definitions emphasized *cultural pluralism* (Grant, 1977), while others focused on *educational equity* (Banks, 1981). More recently *antiracist education and critical pedagogy* (Nieto, 1992) and *freedom* (Banks, 1994) have been included as critical components. In 1995 in the first *Handbook of Research on Multicultural Education*, James and Cherry Banks added the boundary-breaking idea that multicultural education is a fledgling academic discipline (p. xi). This potent conceptual contribution created the view of multicultural education as a movement whose intellectual products and proponents are worthy of a special niche in academia. With a narrower purpose in mind, namely staff development workshops for classroom teachers, Leonard and Patricia Davidman defined multicultural education as a multifaceted change-oriented strategy that is aimed at seven interrelated goals:

1. Educational equity.
2. Empowerment of students and their parents.

3. Cultural pluralism in society.

4. Intergroup and intragroup understanding and harmony in the classroom and school community.

5. An expanded knowledge base of cultural and ethnic groups.

6. The development of students and practitioners (teachers, nurses, administrators, counselors, etc.) whose thoughts and actions are guided by an informed multicultural perspective.

7. Freedom and the maintenance and extension of democracy (2001, p.14).

These goals can be achieved by a wide range of strategies, some of which are included in Figure 10.2; Figure 10.1 provides a visual summary of the preceding synthesis conception.

Despite the inevitable conceptual conflict in the multicultural education literature, which is one outcome of the social construction of knowledge process, almost all writers on this topic agree that multicultural education has been a catalyst for reform in American education and that the 1954 Supreme Court decision in *Brown v. the Board of Education* (of Topeka, Kansas) was a decisive point in this reform movement. The goal of this movement has been to create educational equity for a wide range of cultural and ethnic groups, including women, children with learning disabilities and physical challenges, and more recently gay and lesbian learners, as well as the broad range of students who are targets for bullies. In addition, ethnic groups—cultural groups with a common history—who have been oppressed in American history have always been a focus of advocates of multicultural education. These groups,

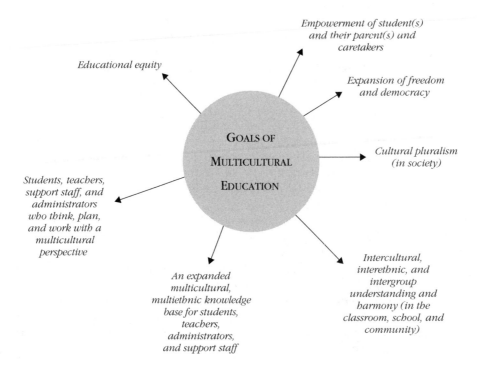

FIGURE 10.1 Goals of Multicultural Education

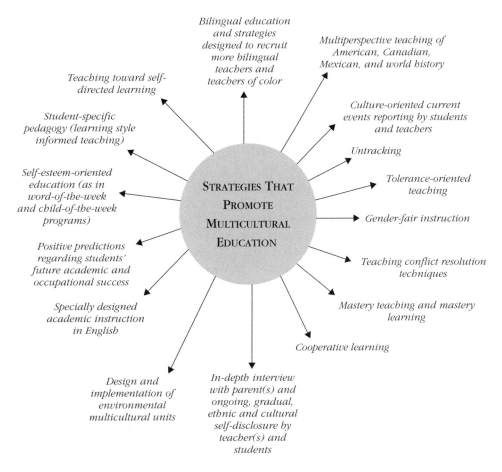

FIGURE 10.2   Strategies That Promote Multicultural Education

which have been differentially impacted by prejudice and racism in American culture, include African Americans, American Indians, and some but not all Hispanic Americans and Asian Americans. James Banks (1981) and others (Gay, 1983) have gone to great lengths to make certain that these groups do not get lost in the variety of groups falling under multicultural education's umbrella of concern. Toward this end, Banks has discussed the concept of *multiethnic education* to complement multicultural education. Multiethnic education complements multicultural education by keeping uppermost in educators' minds the importance of combating racism in American society and all of its manifestations in American schools.

Educational Equity

Educational equity involves the opportunity to study in schools that are equally funded and dedicated to creating optimal academic success for all students. The Davidmans have specifically defined *educational equity* in terms of three observable conditions: physical and financial conditions, the opportunity to learn, and educational outcomes for both individuals and groups (2001, p. 17). Thus when educators strive to create equity in a classroom or school, they try to make the following roughly equivalent (exact numerical equality is a social and bureaucratic impossibility):

1. The physical conditions in which children learn.

2. The quality and experience of teachers and administrators.

3. The opportunity that various types of learners have to learn.

4. Most controversially, the educational achievement of various groups within the class, school, and school district (e.g., boys and girls, black, white, and Hispanic Americans, monolingual and bilingual learners, the economically impoverished and those more fortunate).

Despite the clarity in the preceding definition, creating educational equity in public schools remains elusive, and the concept, for a variety of reasons, remains ambiguous for teachers and administrators. The social construction of knowledge process, because it tends to produce competing conceptions of reality, contributes to the ambiguity, although this need not be the case. When educators understand the knowledge construction process they will better understand both the inevitability of conceptual conflict and their responsibility to work through the confusion with their own critical thinking, definitions, and synthesis conceptions of reality. Let us briefly examine some competing conceptions of educational equity to see how such synthesizing might work.

To begin, we have the theories of the late Kenneth Sirotnick. For Sirotnick, "Equity is concerned with the allocation of resources to *groups*, is assessed quantitatively, and is conceptually linked to the idea of excellence" (Davidman and Davidman, 2001, p. 102). And excellence, Sirotnick notes, is indicated by "conditions, practices, and outcomes in school that are associated with high levels of learning for most students in all valued goal areas of the common curriculum" (1990, p. 159). Based on this perspective, Sirotnick wrote, "Equity is indicated when there are no systematic differences in the distributions of these conditions, practices, and outcomes based upon race, ethnicity, economic status, or any other irrelevant grouping characteristic" (1990, p. 159). When Sirotnick thought about educational equity, he thought about *cultural* and *ethnic groups* and ways to bring the academic achievement of these groups closer together. This perspective is the dominant thinking on educational equity and is a driving force behind the controversial federal legislation known as No Child Left Behind.

In contrast to the group-oriented theories of Sirotnick, we have the equity ideas of Elliot Eisner. Eisner, who constructs his conception of equity from deep within an individualistic perspective, states, "Equity is achieved in education by giving students an opportunity to come to school, but also is influenced by what they find when they arrive. School programs that create a very narrow eye of the needle through which all children must pass diminish educational equity," as well as, "The genuinely good school does not diminish individual differences, it expands them" (1991, p. 17). So we have here two conceptions of educational equity that point us in different directions. One is concerned with diminishing academic achievement differences between racial, gender, and socioeconomic groups; the other is concerned with individual learners and the creation of school curricula that allow these learners to become their own idiosyncratic unique selves and as different as they can possibly become. Although these conceptions can be seen as antithetical, it is also possible that each contains truths that educators can embrace to create schools that are fair both for individuals and for groups that have been oppressed and stigmatized by social forces such as racism, sexism, and homophobia. Indeed, teachers in American society, who deal with *real* individuals in all of their diversity and real social groups in all of their complexity, need "more than an either–or conception of equity. They need a conception that helps them to work wisely and fairly with both individuals and groups and a philosophy that enables them to do this without trampling on the constitutional rights of individuals or groups" (Davidman and Davidman, 2001, p. 104).

We believe that the conception of educational equity that teachers in our society need will flexibly draw upon Eisner and Sirotnick, will include quantitative and qualitative elements such as those discussed by Geneva Gay (1993, p. 189), but will also need new ideas and practices to advance the equity agenda. We all need to see equity as beginning not with schools and *educational* equity, but rather with society and social equity (or social justice)—ultimately integrating educational equity and social justice in a manner that is meaningful for classroom teachers. This integrated conception will remind teachers that it is society that creates fair schools and not the other way around, and that it is futile to focus exclusively on school-based equity issues in a society in which inequality is a deep, relatively unexamined structural value. In other words, guided by the integrated conception, teachers will be challenged to simultaneously work on equity and fairness issues in society *and* school. When they do this, they will face strategies and controversies related to *bilingual education* and *special education*.

Bilingual and Special Education

On a national scale bilingual education and special education are key components of the equity, or fairness, movement. Furthermore, at the classroom level of operation both can be construed as legislated teaching strategies that help to achieve specific goals of multicultural education, most notably educational equity and empowerment of students and parents. Although the relationships among multicultural education, special education, and bilingual education are clear to many, you will also encounter situations where the autonomy of special education and bilingual education is emphasized. This occurs primarily because each was created by federal legislation. In 1973 in *Lau v. Nichols*, a class action suit filed on behalf of Chinese-speaking students in San Francisco schools, the U.S. Supreme Court ruled that schools must provide special language programs for students who don't understand or speak English and that these special programs must not include sink-or-swim submersion as the only alternative available. In a 1975 landmark decision that affected every school and school district in the nation and reverberates to this day, Congress passed Public Law (PL) 94-142, Education for All Handicapped Children. This law stipulated that students with disabilities must be educated in the environment that is least restrictive to their learning. In the decades following this pioneering legislation Congress has added amendments to the original legislation; in 1990 in PL 101-476 it changed the name of the law to the Individuals with Disabilities Education Act.

Individuals with Disabilities Education Act (IDEA)

Since 1990 IDEA has been reauthorized and amended several times. Because the most recent reauthorization and amendments were disseminated in 2004, in our remarks here we refer to IDEA/2004. Regarding the three decades of federal special education legislation, it is noteworthy that despite the many successes attributable to PL 94-142 (1975–1990) and IDEA (1990–2005), there remains in some quarters a thick residue of disappointment. Thus in Section 1400(c)(4) of IDEA/2004 we read that "The implementation of this title (PL 94-142 and IDEA) has been impeded by low expectations and an insufficient focus on applying replicable research on proven methods of teaching and learning for children with disabilities" (Turnbull, Huerta, and Stowe, 2006, p. 7). As a result of these perceived obstacles, as well as their own beliefs about what will work, the authors of IDEA/2004 in Section 1400(c)(5) spell out eight solutions. In broad terms these solutions encourage educators to

1. Employ high expectations.
2. Educate children with disabilities in the regular classroom to the maximum extent possible.
3. Strengthen the role and responsibility of parents.
4. Be more efficient in creating interagency collaborative efforts to support the goals of IDEA/2004.
5. Provide high-quality preservice professional development for all personnel who will work with children with disabilities.
6. Make use of whole-school approaches, scientifically based early reading programs, positive behavioral interventions, and early intervention services.
7. Focus resources on teaching and learning with a simultaneous reduction in paperwork.
8. Support the development and use of technology. (Turnbull, Huerta, and Stowe, 2006, pp.7–8)

These eight solutions are augmented and reinforced in IDEA/2004 by the Six Principles, a set of ideas and explanations aimed at increasing the probability that children with disabilities will be educated to their fullest potential, preferably in a mainstream (integrated) classroom. In brief, the Six Principles are zero reject; nondiscriminatory evaluation; appropriate education; least restrictive environment; procedural due process; and parent participation. Here, because of space considerations, we briefly comment on just two of these Six Principles: least restrictive environment and procedural due process.

The Least Restrictive Environment and Procedural Due Process

Regarding the concept and interpretation of the *least restrictive environment* (hereafter LRE), we note first that the LRE was a key element in both the 1975–1990 period (LRE #1) and the 1990–2005 period (LRE #2) and second that there is one critical difference between the ways in which LRE #1 and #2 were interpreted and implemented. With LRE #1 there was no presumption that either of the two main possible learning environments (the integrated regular education classroom or the segregated all-day special education classroom) was the better educational setting for each and every student with a disability. Each case would be analyzed on its own merits, and if the segregated setting was chosen the school site review team was under no special obligation to defend its choice. LRE #2 is a horse of a different color. The Individuals with Disabilities Education Act of 1990 replaced the assumption of neutrality with the general presumption that students with disabilities, like all students, belong in the regular mainstream classroom where they will receive access to the full general education curriculum. In addition, under IDEA/2004 [Section 1414 (d)(1)(A)(i)(V)] if a student with a disability is *not* placed in a regular education classroom, the school site review team must include in the student's individual education plan (IEP) an explanation of the extent to which the student will not participate with nondisabled students in the regular education classroom, the general education curriculum, and extracurricular and other nonacademic activities. Clearly the legal pendulum has swung strongly toward the idea that full inclusion in a regular education classroom *and* the total school environment is the LRE for most students with disabilities. And if full inclusion is not possible, then partial inclusion is considered the most equitable choice for all concerned; the exception would be those whose disability is too severe to benefit from time in the mainstream.

To help ensure that the most equitable choice is made for all we have *procedural due process,* another critical IDEA/2004 principle. Following the deep-rooted United States tradition of checks and balances, this principle incorporates the ideas that (1) for IDEA/2004 to work on behalf of students, parents, and local and state educational agencies, all of these parties should have well-defined rights to protect their interests as necessary, and (2) all of these parties are expected to deal fairly with each other. Toward this end, the framers of this principle actually spell out procedures for fair dealing (Turnbull, Huerta, and Stowe, 2006, p. 71). Further, the due process principle leads us to consider another variable in the fairness equation: the concept of *learning style.*

Learning Styles

When children who fall under the protection of PL 94-142 and PL 101-476 are placed into their least restrictive environment, an individual educational plan (IEP) is drawn up by a team of educators in consultation with the children's parent(s) or caregiver(s). Increasingly, these mandatory IEPs attempt to take into account the students' learning styles and preferences as the school site team identifies specific goals and learning activities for the children in question. As used here, *learning style* refers to the variables that describe how an individual prefers to learn difficult information. When these variables are folded into a child's learning environment, his or her academic aptitude and performance should increase. Examples of learning style variables include the time of day when a child will take a course, the type of lighting in a room, the presence and degree of cooperative learning in a classroom, the opportunity to listen to chapters in a text as opposed to an exclusive reliance on reading, and the presence of a very structured, demanding teacher as opposed to a low-pressure learning environment characterized by lots of opportunity for self-directed learning. Many students will benefit from one or more of these variables but can be successful learners without them. For such learners the variables are *instructional preferences.* In contrast, for other learners the presence or absence of a variable will have a more dramatic effect. It is when these variables are almost a biological or cultural need that they are properly perceived as part of an individual's deep learning style.

Bilingual Education—English Language Development

Bilingual education in the contemporary curriculum, as noted earlier, was given legal support by the U.S. Supreme Court in 1973; but it has been a part of American public education since the nineteenth century when German-speaking students received daily instruction in English and German. Today the term *bilingual education* means many things, but at a general level it is best understood "as an educational program that involves the use of two languages of instruction at some point in a student's school career" (Nieto, 1992). The recipient is typically, but not always, a second language learner who (in America) is learning English as a second language. In the upside-down world of education, when English speakers (in America) learn a second language, the process is typically referred to as foreign language instruction, unless, of course, it is the student's native tongue.

Some of the major types of bilingual education are transitional bilingual education, maintenance bilingual education, and bilingual/bicultural education. In the *maintenance* approach the goal is to produce students who will be functionally bilingual, whereas in the *transitional* approach students move into an English-only program as soon as possible with no consideration given to bilingualism. In either process, when the learners' native culture as well as language are made part of the curriculum, the approach is sometimes called *bilingual/bicultural education* (Nieto, 1992).

The critical point is that bilingual education—and related terms like *English language learner* (ELL), *English language development* (ELD), *specially designed academic instruction in English* (SDAIE), and *limited English proficient* (LEP)—points to a significant dimension of diversity in our nation. The current wave of immigration into the United States is bringing hundreds of thousands of English language learners into the classes that you will teach. These new Americans are coming into schools that no longer try to melt away *all* of their cultural differences. Indeed, utilization of these differences, a strong emphasis on English literacy, and a weaker emphasis on bilingualism are part of the complex equation of multicultural education. This is an equation to which you will inevitably contribute, and the sooner you sort out your attitudes, the better. Parenthetically, with attitudes in mind, it is instructive that educators in certain states, like California, now use the term *English learner* rather than *limited English proficient*. They believe that the former has less negative connotation.

Gifted and Talented and At-Risk Learners

Another controversial term associated with individual differences in aptitude and academic performance is *gifted and talented*. Often perceived as part of the special education continuum, gifted and talented programs try to create optimal learning environments for students whose intellectual aptitude and rate of learning are extraordinarily high. Some educators believe that these students are penalized when they are kept exclusively in the regular education program with students and teachers who possess a different intellectual capacity. Special yearlong residential (live-away) public schools for scientifically and mathematically talented students are one example of a program for the gifted and talented; high school programs that facilitate study at local and distant universities via computers and other means are another.

Finally, we have a term invented in the 1980s, namely the *at-risk learner*. At-risk learners are students whose poor academic achievement (typically in reading and math) flags them as students who are likely to drop out. Federal and state dollars support at-risk programs, and increasingly we find special tutorial programs for such learners beginning as early as the first grade (Pinnell, Fried, and Estice, 1990). Although the term *at risk* did not exist in the 1960s, the Head Start program, which gave preschoolers nutritional and academic support, was and still is a program designed to support at-risk learners. Furthermore, in contemporary American schools we have recognized a relatively new type of at-risk student: one who is repeatedly harassed by school bullies. *Bullying* has been defined as being "exposed, repeatedly and over time, to negative actions on the part of one or more students" (Olweus, 1991). Survey data collected in 2001 and summarized in 2005 clearly suggest that bullying of target pupils is a serious matter worthy of consideration in teacher preparation programs and beyond (Chandler, DeVoe, and Kaffenberger, 2005) For example, Chandler and colleagues (pp. vi–vii) report in their executive summary that

1. 14 percent of students aged 12 through 18 reported that they had been bullied at school in the six months prior to the interview.
2. Younger students were more likely than older students to report being bullied (24 percent of sixth graders reported bullying incidents as opposed to 7 percent of twelfth graders).
3. Victims of bullying were more afraid of being attacked at school and elsewhere (18 percent of bullied students feared being attacked at school as opposed to 3 percent of nonbullied students).
4. Victims of bullying were more likely to report that they carried weapons to school for protection (4 percent of bullied students reported carrying weapons versus 1 percent of the nonbullied).
5. Victims of bullying were more likely to report receiving D and F grades than nonbullied students (8 percent versus 3 percent).

MEETING THE CHALLENGE OF DIVERSITY

Clearly one of the greatest challenges that you will experience as a teacher will stem from your attempt to sensitively and wisely respond to the diversity of sociocultural backgrounds and instructional needs among your students. Your ability to respond appropriately to this challenge will be strongly influenced by your knowledge base and attitudes regarding diversity. Traditionally, when considering a career in teaching, prospective teachers—particularly those oriented toward elementary teaching—have been asked to consider whether they really like children. An equally valid question for today's prospective teacher is: Will you welcome, value, and promote diversity in your classroom? At this point in your professional development this broad question will not be easy to answer, but you can gain some insight into your feelings about diversity by completing the activities that follow.

Note that the Core Activity specifies a certain type of classroom for observation. In some areas of the United States such integrated classrooms will be difficult to locate. Our fundamental objective is to have prospective teachers observe teachers who respond to diversity in an exemplary manner. The degree of specific ethnic diversity is less important than the expertise manifested by the teacher. Also, we appreciate that some teacher education programs operate almost totally in environments that are rich in diversity. We hope that in such areas the activities that follow will reinforce and extend the normal pattern of preservice observation.

Finally, beyond the following activities, you can take two steps that will help you develop a multicultural knowledge base and pluralistic attitude. First, seek information regarding professional organizations that are committed to clarifying and advancing the multicultural education agenda. Currently the preeminent such organization is the National Association for Multicultural Education (NAME). This organization, which came into existence in 1991, has been developing statewide chapters since 1996 so that members can now participate in state and national meetings and projects. The organization publishes *Proceedings* from its annual meetings and a quarterly magazine titled *Multicultural Perspectives.* Membership dues for NAME in 2005 were $75 per year for regular members and $40 per year for students, and this included a subscription to *Multicultural Perspectives.* For specific membership information contact the NAME national office at (202)628-6263, or 733 15th Street NW, Suite 430, Washington, DC, 20005, or via e-mail at name@nameorg.org.

The second step is to subscribe to a listserv (e-mail discussion group) concerned with multicultural education. One worthy of your attention, NAME-MCE, is hosted by NAME. This listserv provides a forum to discuss multicultural education, announce conferences or other events, and pose questions to educators and activists around the world. Questions regarding this listserv should be addressed to listmoderator @nameorg.org. To subscribe to NAME-MCE, send an e-mail message to listserv.umd.edu with the subject line blank and the following in the body of the message: Subscribe NAME-MCE [first name last name]. For example, if your name is Mary Lamb, you would enter the following: Subscribe NAME-MCE Mary Lamb. You will receive a confirmation of your subscription and listserv instructions via e-mail.

The best print resource for locating information about other multicultural-oriented organizations, Web sites, and discussion groups (and much more) is the second edition of *Multicultural Education and the Internet: Intersections and Integrations* by Paul C. Gorski (McGraw-Hill, 2005, ISBN 0073011436). In August 2005 the book sold for under $16.00.

Core Activity

OBSERVING DIVERSITY IN THE CLASSROOM

Observe for a full day or two half days in an upper-level (fourth, fifth, or sixth grade, junior high, or high school) classroom that has a rich diversity of ethnic and racial groups (approximately 50 percent nonwhite, if possible) as well as several English language learners who receive regular ELD or SDAIE instruction. The teacher you observe should be identified as a successful teacher by your professor, and if possible the classroom should be in a school considered to be lower SES (socioeconomic status) in the school district. After your observation, do the following:

1. Answer these questions:
   a. How would you feel if you were assigned to teach in this classroom?
   b. Would you want to teach in this classroom? In this school? Why or why not?
   c. What questions would you like to ask the teacher? Why?
2. Conduct an informal, semistructured interview with the teacher and/or the principal of the school. Try to discuss how the teacher and/or principal
   a. Thinks and feels about the classroom or schoolwide diversity that he or she encounters.
   b. Defines *multicultural education* and/or teaching with a multicultural perspective.
   c. Feels about the federal legislation known as No Child Left Behind.

Write a few paragraphs that compare and contrast your interviewee's perceptions of classroom diversity and multicultural education with those presented in this chapter. Where possible, discuss your findings with other prospective teachers.

Suggested Activity 1

OBSERVING MULTICULTURAL SETTINGS

Observe for a full day or two half days in a classroom that mirrors the following characteristics as closely as possible. The school in which you observe should be considered a predominantly middle-class school by the principal.

1. Predominantly middle-class students.
2. 20–75 percent visibly ethnic students (African American, Hispanic American, Native American, or Asian American).
3. Several students with learning disabilities who are fully integrated.

After this observation, complete the following activities:

1. Answer these questions:
   a. Did the teaching, learning, classroom environment, and classroom interaction in this setting differ from those of the classroom that you observed in your Core Activity? Did they differ from other classrooms where you have observed? What, if any, were the most significant differences?
   b. How would you feel if you were assigned to teach in this classroom? Would you want to teach in this classroom? This school? Why or why not?
2. Conduct an informal, semistructured interview with the teacher and/or the principal of the school. Try to discover how the teacher and/or principal
   a. Feels about the level of classroom or schoolwide diversity with which she or he works.
   b. Feels about policies associated with IDEA/2004, particularly those associated with full inclusion.
   c. Orients teaching and evaluation toward a better match with students' special learning styles.
   d. Views and defines *multicultural education* and/or teaching with a multicultural perspective.

Write a few paragraphs that compare and contrast your interviewee's perceptions of multicultural education with those presented in this chapter. Does your interviewee make a connection between multicultural education and special education (the education that students with disabilities and other "exceptional" children receive)? Where possible, discuss your findings with other prospective teachers.

Suggested Activity 2

OBSERVING THE SPECIAL NEEDS CLASSROOM

Most elementary, junior high, and high schools have special teachers who work individually or in small groups in special rooms with learners who have special needs. Typically the teachers who provide this instruction have received training to prepare them for this challenging role, which includes providing "special education support" for the regular classroom teachers in the school. For the purpose of learning how to deal with diversity in the classroom, these resource rooms or special educators can be a valuable resource for prospective teachers. To tap into this resource, perform the following:

1. Observe in a resource room for an entire morning, noting the physical differences between the resource classroom and the regular classroom. What resources does the special education room have that the regular classroom doesn't? In addition, observe and take notes on how the resource room teacher interacts with students. (Note that in your region or state the resource room may have a different name. Seek out the room where individualized instruction is provided for students with special learning needs.)

2. If possible, observe for an entire morning in a classroom where the resource room teacher helps the regular classroom teacher in the latter's classroom. This will occasionally occur when a severely challenged learner is placed into a mainstream classroom.

3. Conduct an informal, semistructured interview with the resource room teacher. Try to discover
   a. If the resource room teacher uses learning style data or any other type of special information in designing effective instruction for her or his students.
   b. What the resource room teacher believes the regular classroom teacher can do in his or her own classroom to create supportive, enabling learning environments for learners with special needs.
   c. If the resource room teacher believes that specific teaching strategies or approaches to teaching would benefit most of the children she or he teaches.
   d. If the school district has any special projects that involve partial inclusion of students with severe disabilities—and if so, what the resource room teacher thinks about these projects.

4. Write a few paragraphs that summarize what you have learned about creating supportive, enabling learning environments for students with special learning needs. Where possible, discuss your findings with other prospective teachers.

Suggested Activity 3

OBSERVING LEARNING/TEACHING STYLES

It is widely assumed that teachers who are adept at creating supportive, enabling learning environments for diverse students can do so because they have developed a flexible teaching style. They have developed an ability and commitment to flex toward the diverse learning styles and needs of their students. Sometimes the ability to flex begins with a heightened awareness of one's own learning style. Completing the following worksheet, followed by class or small-group discussions, should be an illuminating exercise.

The learning and teaching style analysis worksheet has been used in a variety of teacher education courses (Davidman, 1984). The worksheet is filled out after several conceptions of learning style are discussed. The learning style conceptions of James Renzulli, Linda Smith, Rita Dunn, and Gary Price, although different, have served as useful stimuli for teachers' self-analysis of their own learning styles. Renzulli and Smith define *learning style* in terms of the teaching strategies by which students prefer to learn. The strategies presented in their instrument are these:

Projects	Independent study
Drill and recitation	Programmed instruction
Peer teaching	Lecture
Discussion	Simulation
Teaching games	

The Dunn/Price conception and instrument, on the other hand, incorporates a wide range of variables that affect how learners concentrate on, absorb, and retain new or difficult information and skills. The variables, which are listed next, are environmental, sociological, physical, and psychological. The wide-ranging Dunn/Price conception is valuable because it reminds us that for some learners an environmental variable like light or warmth may be as critical to learning success as is a specific teaching strategy. The Dunn/Price variables are these:

Prefers learning through several ways	Light
Auditory preferences	Warmth
Visual preferences	Formal design
Tactile preferences	Motivated/unmotivated
Kinesthetic preferences	Adult motivated
Requires intake	Teacher motivated
Functions best in morning	Persistent
Functions best in late morning	Responsible
Functions best in afternoon	Structure
Functions best in evening	Prefers learning alone
Needs mobility	Peer-oriented learner
Sound	Learning with adults

INSTRUCTIONS

Before you fill in the following worksheet, try to identify some of the best and worst learning experiences you've had in the past five or so years. Then, as you complete these sentences, use these learning experiences as a source of data. In addition, for items 1 through 3, think about school and home learning environments, paying particular attention to the teachers' strategies, structure of the class, and any cognitive, affective, or environmental variables that you consider pertinent. Refer to the preceding Dunn/Price and Renzulli/Smith lists as you complete this form. Complete items 7 and 8 only if you have had teaching experience.

Student Name: _____ Date: _____

LEARNING AND TEACHING STYLE ANALYSIS WORKSHEET

1. I learn new and/or difficult information best when

    a. _____

    b. _____

    c. _____

    d. _____

    e. _____

    f. _____

    g. _____

2. I have trouble learning new and/or difficult information when

    a. _____

    b. _____

    c. _____

    d. _____

    e. _____

    f. _____

    g. _____

3. I find it *very* helpful to my learning if the learning environment is or has

    a. _____

    b. _____

    c. _____

    d. _____

    e. _____

    f. _____

    g. _____

Student Name: _____ Date: _____

4. When I study, whether at home or at school, I like to

   a. _____

   b. _____

   c. _____

   d. _____

   e. _____

   f _____

5. The way that I learn is probably like that of others in many ways, but I think that it may be special because I

   a. _____

   b. _____

   c. _____

6. Between elementary school and today, my learning style preferences/needs have
   ❏ Remained pretty much the same.
   ❏ Changed moderately (please describe the changes here).
   ❏ Changed a great deal (please describe the changes here).

   _____

   _____

   _____

   _____

   _____

   _____

   _____

   _____

   _____

Student Name: _____   Date: _____

7. Regarding my teaching style, in my teaching I will likely make good use of the following teaching strategies (or would if the resources were available). Put an *X* into the boxes in front of the appropriate strategies, and fill in your own strategies if they are not here:

❑ Discussion
❑ Lectures (or minilectures)
❑ Drill and recitation
❑ Computer-assisted instruction
❑ Independent study
❑ Simulations
❑ Directed reading
❑ Learning centers

❑ Programmed instruction
❑ Games
❑ The project approach
❑ Peer tutoring
❑ Direct instruction
❑ Discovery learning
❑ Listening posts

Student Name: _____ Date: _____

8. Regarding a possible connection between my current learning style and my current teaching style, at this point I

❑ See no connection.

❑ See one or more possible connections (please describe here).

_____

_____

_____

_____

_____

_____

_____

_____

_____

_____

_____

_____

_____

_____

_____

_____

_____

_____

_____

_____

_____

_____

_____

_____

Suggested Activity 4

OBSERVING SPECIALLY DESIGNED ACADEMIC INSTRUCTION IN ENGLISH (SDAIE)

Although bilingual instruction (maintenance and transitional) is increasingly accepted as the most appropriate teaching strategy for English language learners, in many school settings it is difficult to provide enough teachers who are fluent in the learners' first language. For these learners, as well as for learners who are receiving dual language instruction, a special and sensible approach to teaching the new language (English) has evolved. The approach is called *specially designed academic instruction in English (SDAIE)*, and the basic idea is to use a variety of strategies to make English communication in core academic subjects such as science, math, and social studies as comprehensible as possible. For example, teachers using SDAIE usually simplify their language by using shorter sentences, speaking more slowly, and avoiding ambiguous vocabulary and idioms such as "Don't use off-the-wall ideas!" In addition, they make greater use of visual aids, hand gestures, physical props, and manipulatives. General knowledge of second language acquisition also comes into play as instructors employing SDAIE create low-stress learning environments and welcome their students' attempts to maintain the use of their native language. There is much more to SDAIE, and it is our hope that the following observation task will stimulate your growth in this important area.

THE OBSERVATION TASK

With the help of your instructor, identify several classrooms where SDAIE is employed and observe several lessons if possible.

1. If possible, observe a teacher whose students speak three or more different languages and are in their first year of learning English. Typically this teacher will not be fluent in any of the native languages spoken by the students.

2. As a contrast, attempt to observe a bilingual teacher who is working with students at various levels of English proficiency. If time permits, interview both teachers regarding their perspectives on SDAIE and bilingual education.

SDAIE OBSERVATION FORM

Name: _____ Teacher: _____

Date: _____ Grade/Subject: _____

School: _____

Data Collection

1. Specifically, what did the teacher do to make his or her oral remarks comprehensible to the English language learners in his or her class?

_____

_____

_____

_____

2. How did her or his oral and nonverbal communication differ from communication that you have observed in other classrooms?

_____

_____

_____

_____

3. Did this teacher use cooperative learning groups or partners to increase student comprehension of instructions and lesson content? If so, how did the groups or partners appear to be functioning?

_____

_____

_____

_____

4. What, if anything, did you notice about the teacher's use of visual aids, manipulatives, or special props?

_____

_____

_____

_____

5. Beyond the variables already mentioned, what else did the teacher do to increase the comprehensibility of the lesson content?

_____

_____

_____

_____

6. How would you describe the reaction of the English language learners to SDAIE?

_____

_____

_____

_____

_____

Comparison, Contrast, and Analysis

1. Based on your observation(s) and possible interview(s), how would you describe the differences between SDAIE and other approaches to effective instruction with which you are familiar? How would you describe the commonalities?

_____

_____

_____

_____

_____

_____

2. What were the significant differences between the SDAIE classroom and other classrooms that you have recently observed?

_____

_____

_____

_____

_____

3. What did you like about the teaching that you observed? What, if anything appeared dubious to you? What questions do you have about SDAIE?

_____

_____

_____

_____

_____

Student Name:_____   Date:_____

Journal Entry

Because this chapter focused on accepting or embracing the challenge of diversity and individual differences, your Journal Entry should concentrate on what you have learned about

1. Yourself and your own potential to work with a diverse student population.
2. Your desire to modify instruction to meet individual students' needs.
3. Your own thoughts and feelings about multicultural education, special education, bilingual education, SDAIE, and other types of supportive learning environments.
4. Your own learning and (potential) teaching styles.

_____

_____

_____

_____

_____

_____

_____

_____

_____

_____

_____

_____

_____

_____

_____

_____

_____

_____

Questions for Discussion

1. The authors assert that commitment to diversity, which implies a pervasive and consistent attention to individual differences, is a part of the tradition, symbolic rhetoric, and legislative framework of American education, and is what gives the American classroom special standing among the classrooms of the world.

   a. Do you agree with these assertions? Why or why not?

   b. If you don't totally agree with these assertions, to what extent do you believe that they are accurate?

2. What connections do you see between *special education* and *multicultural education*? Where do these terms overlap and diverge?

3. In discussing learning style–informed education, some practitioners have charged that it is not practical. "You just can't customize a learning environment for every learner in the class." What is your reaction to this assertion?

4. What are your thoughts about the following statement, which comments on the flexibility and teaching style of a multicultural educator?

   > By definition a multicultural educator's teaching style should be strongly influenced by the learning styles and learning needs of her students. She may enjoy teaching and learning in highly individualistic, competitive learning environments, love to lecture, and know and care very little about the history and demography of Mexico. But if research or teacher experience has demonstrated that cooperative learning groups, high degrees of student active participation and discussion, and teacher knowledge of Mexican history have proven to be beneficial to the learning of her students, the multicultural educator will modify her teaching style to move in the direction of her students' learning styles and needs.

5. This chapter implies that a supportive/enabling classroom teacher will, among other things, strive to countervail and diminish the effects of racism, sexism, bullying, handicaps, and religious and sexual orientation intolerance in our society by positively responding to diversity and individual differences in his or her instruction.

   a. Do you think that this is an appropriate and realistic task for classroom teachers? Why or why not?

   b. As a future educator, how would you describe your own feelings about the various "*isms*" just mentioned? Do these words, for example, represent forces that contemporary educators should be knowledgeable about, or are they divisive topics worthy of minimal attention in an education program?

References

Banks, J.A. (1981). *Multiethnic education: Theory and practice* (p. 32). Boston: Allyn and Bacon.

Banks, J.A. (1994). *An introduction to multicultural education* (pp. 16–17). Needham Heights: Allyn and Bacon.

Banks, J.A., and Banks, C.A. (1995). *Handbook of research on multicultural education*. New York: Macmillan.

Chandler, K., Devoe, J. F., and Kaffenberger, S. (2005). *Student reports of bullying: Results from the 2001 school crime supplement to the national Crime Victimization Survey (NCES 2005310)*. Washington, DC: U.S. Dept. of Education, National Center for Education Statistics. U.S. Government Printing Office.

Davidman, L. (1984). *Learning style and teaching style analysis in the teacher education curriculum: A synthesis approach*. ERIC Document Reproduction Service No. ED 249183.

Davidman, L., and Davidman, P. (2001). *Teaching with a multicultural perspective: A practical guide* (3rd ed.). White Plains, NY: Longman.

Douglas-Hall, A., and Koball, H. (2004). *Rate of children in low-income families varies widely by state*. New York: National Center for Children in Poverty. www.nccp.org.

Douglas-Hall, A., and Koball, H. (2005). *Basic facts about low-income children in the United States*. New York: National Center for Children in Poverty, Columbia University's Mailman School of Public Health.

Eisner, E. W. (1991). What really counts in schools. *Educational Leadership, 48(5)*.

Gay, G. (1983). Multiethnic education: Historical development and future prospects. *Phi Delta Kappan 65(8)*.

Gay, G. (1993). Ethnic minorities and educational equality. In J. A. Banks and C. A. Banks (Eds.), *Multicultural education: Issues and perspectives* (2nd ed.). Boston: Allyn and Bacon.

Gorski, P.C. (2005). *Multicultural education and the Internet: Intersections and integrations* (2nd ed.). Boston: McGraw-Hill.

Grant, C. A. (Ed.). (1977). *Multicultural education: Commitments, issues, and applications* (p. 2). Washington, DC: The Association for Supervision and Curriculum Development.

Nieto, S. (1992). *Affirming diversity: The sociopolitical context of multicultural education*. White Plains, NY: Longman.

Olweus, D. (1991). Bully/victim problems among schoolchildren: Some basic facts and effects of a school-based intervention program. In D. Pepler and K. Rubin (Eds.), *The development and treatment of childhood aggression*. Hillsdale, NJ: Earlbaum.

Pinnell, G. S., Fried, M. D., and Estice, R. M. (1990). Reading recovery: Learning how to make a difference. *The Reading Teacher, 43(4)*, 282–295.

Sirotnick, K. (1990). Equal access to quality in public schooling: Issues in the assessment of equality and excellence. In J. I. Goodlad and P. Keating (Eds.), *Access to knowledge: An agenda for our nation's schools*. New York: The College Board.

Tetreault, M. (1993). Classrooms for diversity: Rethinking curriculum and pedagogy. In J.A. Banks and C.A. Banks (Eds.), *Multicultural education: Issues and perspectives* (2nd ed.). Boston: Allyn and Bacon.

Turnbull, II. R., Huerta, N., and Stowe, M. (2006). *The Individuals with Disabilities Education Act as amended in 2004* (2nd ed.). Old Tappan, NJ: Prentice-Hall.

U.S. Dept. of Education Office of Elementary and Secondary Education. (2000). *Education for homeless children and youth program—Report to Congress, fiscal year 2000*. www.ed.gov/program/homeless/rpt2000.doc.

The United States Interagency Council on Homelessness e-newsletter (2004). Federal Partner Profile: U.S. Dept. of Education, Washington DC. www.ich.gov/newsletter/archive/05-20-04_e-newsletter.htm.

General Multicultural Education Resources

Banks, J.A., et al. (2001). *Diversity within unity: Essential principles for teaching and learning in a multicultural society*. Seattle: Center for Multicultural Education (College of Education, University of Washington).

Banks, J.A., et al. (2005). *Democracy and diversity: Principles and concepts for educating citizens in a global age*. Seattle: Center for Multicultural Education (College of Education, University of Washington).

Banks, J.A. (Ed.), and Banks, C.A. McGee (Assoc. Ed.). (2004). *Handbook of research on multicultural education* (2nd ed.). San Francisco: Jossey-Bass.

Chapter 11

ON BECOMING A TEACHER

And so we will end with you. This book has been designed as a travel book, intended to take you on a journey. Instead of purchasing an airline ticket or signing up for a cruise, you took a course designed to introduce you to the field of education and the world of schools. Of course, our readers are not strangers to school, most having spent a large portion of their lives in one classroom or another. However, this journey was a "backstage tour," an opportunity for you to see students and schools through the eyes of the teachers—if you will, from the other side of the footlights.

You have been the reporter, the observer, the stranger in a not-so-strange land. You have looked at familiar objects through new lenses. You have recorded classroom behavior and tried in various ways to capture and thus better understand what goes on in schools. You have questioned children and adults about their experiences. You have seen yourself—three or thirteen years earlier—in some of those students. Old memories have been evoked by the smell of the school cafeteria and the empty gymnasium. The purpose of this journey, this backstage trip through school, has not been to simply gather facts, to learn how to use observational instruments, or to learn a few perspectives on education. Nor has it been a mere sentimental journey.

Henry David Thoreau, one of our most distinguished essayists and a crusty observer of life, once said of travel, "It is not worthwhile to go around the world to count the cats in Zanzibar." In other words, travel can be a potent type of educational experience; it should do something to us and for us. We should be changed as a result of the travel, seeing ourselves and our world differently as a result of observing life in Zanzibar or in P.S. 22. We will have wasted our time and money if we just collected facts—or worse, if we passively experienced the journey like a film that we really weren't interested in seeing or talking about. The purpose of this chapter, then, is to help you think about your journey, putting what you have learned into perspective.

Having given you information and insights into classrooms and the people who inhabit them, we turn now to a different focus. Socrates once proclaimed that the aim of education is to "know thyself." How has your work in this course deepened your understanding of yourself? Has it clarified your understanding of what is involved in teaching? Has it given you a richer sense of what is involved? Has it helped you to answer the questions "Is teaching for you?" and "Are you for teaching?" Some of you may already have solid answers to these questions; but most of you, we suspect, will benefit from one final set of thought-provoking observation and analysis activities as you attempt to develop clearer answers to these questions. However, now, as your journey in this course is nearing completion, *you* will become the object of observation and analysis. And the observation activities that follow, like many others in this text, will give you tools that will prove valuable to you in journeys that reach far beyond this course. The self-observation/analysis activities that follow will lead you into a personal goal/objective-setting activity that we hope will be the beginning of your career as an active, analytical, self-directed professional.

Core Activity
MAKING YOURSELF A TEACHER

The great majority of people who teach children go through a carefully sequenced program of academic and professional courses. They are said to "have gone through" teacher education. They have been "prepared." In one sense, this is correct. But in another, it is misleading. To "go through" teacher education and to "be prepared" are much too passive a description of what ought to happen.

Becoming a good teacher, like becoming a good musician or a good athlete, requires much self-initiative and self-direction. Training helps. Courses are important. Ultimately, however, the teacher makes himself or herself a good teacher. In effect, the individual is both the maker and the made, both the artist and the work of art. Such a point of view requires the maker—the future teacher—to have both the will to make the changes and the idea of what he or she is making. By "will" we mean the desire and persistence to work toward the goals of becoming a skilled and dedicated teacher. By "idea" we mean a clear vision of what is being made, a blueprint that guides your activity. For instance, if a prospective teacher discovers that he is shy, he needs to overcome this condition. He needs to put himself into situations where he is forced to reach out to others and begins to be comfortable in the rather public role of the teacher. Or if a prospective teacher is a big talker but a poor listener, she needs to learn how to limit her talking, ask more questions, and carefully and patiently listen to what others are saying.

Developing the will is essential, but it is beyond the scope of this book. However, it is our intention to assist you in developing some of the ideas that should guide your efforts to make yourself a teacher. To do this, we urge you to complete three final steps.

First, review all of your answers to the exercises in this book with an eye toward identifying areas of strength and areas needing your attention. (If you have not completed all of the exercises, complete them before going any further.)

Second, after you have done the review, list your strengths and areas needing your attention in specific terms. This is an important step, and you need to take time and give your full attention to it.

AREAS OF STRENGTH

1. _____

2. _____

3. _____

4. _____

5. _____

6. _____

7. _____

8. _____

9. _____

10. _____

11. _____

12. _____

AREAS NEEDING ATTENTION

1. _____

2. _____

3. _____

4. _____

5. _____

6. _____

7. _____

8. _____

9. _____

10. _____

11. _____

12. _____

Third, and finally, you need to develop some specific goals. Because none of us will ever be "the perfect teacher" and because we will always need to find ways to improve, we are not suggesting that you identify everything that you need to reach such a never-ending goal. Rather, we want you to state in quite specific terms what you believe are five objectives that will bring you closer to becoming a good teacher. These five objectives should be based on what you have done earlier; they should be realistic, practical, and attainable objectives. For instance, "Making myself a great math teacher" is much too general. So, too, is "Getting over being shy." A more appropriate objective might be "I will learn to maintain eye contact with people while speaking to them." Or "I will learn to listen carefully to what people are saying to me, or so that if I have to, I can repeat it back to them."

Objective 1: _____

_____

Objective 2: _____

_____

Objective 3: _____

_____

Objective 4: _____

_____

Objective 5: _____

_____

The important point is that these are *your* objectives and that you use them to guide your efforts at making yourself the best teacher that you are capable of becoming.

This goal, though, of "becoming the best teacher that you are capable of becoming," is definitely not a one-shot effort. Implicit in the message of this text is that you must become a "reflective practitioner." One thing we can be sure of: A classroom teacher gets a great deal of practice! Compared to a surgeon who may operate one or two days a week or a trial lawyer who spends three or four days a month in the courtroom, a teacher's "practice time" is immense. In fact, there is so much practice—so much asking of questions, explaining of ideas, managing of classroom routines—that it is difficult for teachers to step back and actually "see" what they are doing.

Regrettably, as many golfers and tennis players know well, "practice does not make perfect." Practice may just reinforce bad habits, such as always calling on the most prepared students, or chattering on when we should be asking questions, or allowing small classroom misbehaviors to sprout into bigger problems. To break the cycle of poor or mediocre practice, we recommend reflective practice—the process of examination and evaluation in which you develop the habit of inquiry and reflection. Although this sounds formidable, reflective practice simply means spending time and energy thinking about and trying to understand what you are doing in the classroom. It means devoting part of your day to going over what you intended to do and what you actually did, making a judgment of how well it worked or didn't work, and then thinking of alternative ways to do it (Dewey, 1938). Some teachers do this on their own. Some involve partners, who occasionally observe their classrooms to provide an objective view. Some reflective practitioners have found it useful to keep a journal, while others have had themselves videotaped. Some work with groups of teachers to write critical incident protocols, in which teachers share classroom stories and together analyze the dynamics of events (Tripp, 1993). There are many roads to being a reflective practitioner, but all involve a commitment to taking a regular and candid look at one's teaching and then taking steps toward improvement. Being a professional teacher requires being a reflective practitioner.

Suggested Activity 1
KNOWING THYSELF

Winston Churchill, who many people think was the greatest statesman of the past century, once described Russia as an enigma wrapped in a mystery. So, too, is the self, but few of us recognize this. If we reflect upon who we are for a moment, we can come up with words or ideas that describe or explain ourselves. But this description or explanation is probably a superficial view. Would our parents come up with the same description? Would our best friends or roommates see us the same way? Would a psychologist probing our unconscious simply confirm our own list of words and ideas?

One way to look at ourselves, to approximate who we are, is to think of certain dimensions of self. This approach has been conceptualized in the famous Johari Window. In it the self is divided into four panes of a window.

The first pane, called the *Arena*, represents that part of self that is known to both ourselves and to others. It is that part of the self that we present to the public that we recognize, and of which we take ownership. This is familiar territory.

Self

	Things I Know	Things I Don't Know
Things They Know	Arena	Blind Spot
Others Things They Don't Know	Private Self	Mystery

The second pane (moving down) is the *Private Self*. Here is the self that we typically keep secret but that we might under special circumstances share with someone close to us. Often our fears and insecurities, our doubts and secret ambitions and passions, are hidden here.

The third pane (upper right) is called the *Blind Spot*. This is the self that others see but that we don't see. Contained here is a self that, if revealed to us, would surprise us. Sometimes the Blind Spot contains pleasant characteristics, sometimes unpleasant characteristics. It is not unlike a person with a sign pinned to the back of his or her coat that everyone else can read.

The fourth pane is called the *Mystery*. Here is the self that neither we nor outside observers are aware of. It is completely hidden from view, but it may be a strong force in our lives. It may contain dreams and passions and fantasies of which we are not consciously aware. It is our mystery, and although we may come to know more of it, the mystery will never disappear (Luft, 1970).

During the next few days, complete your own Johari Window. To do this, follow these steps:

First, list five adjectives or phrases that you would use to describe yourself accurately to others:

1. _____
2. _____
3. _____
4. _____
5. _____

Second, list five adjectives or phrases that you feel someone else who knows you well would use to describe you:

1. _____
2. _____
3. _____
4. _____
5. _____

Third, choose a roommate or classmate who, you believe, knows you well and ask that person to thoughtfully list five adjectives or phrases that describe you, but about which you are most likely unaware:

1. _____
2. _____

3. _____

4. _____

5. _____

Fourth, compare the lists. What have these three angles of viewing you revealed? What are the similarities in the lists? What are the differences? How do you explain the differences? Think about what you have learned about yourself from the exercise so far.

Fifth, your instructor may or may not choose to put you into small groups to go over what you have learned in the first four steps. At this point, however, you should fill in as fully as you can your own Johari Window.

QUESTIONS

1. What happened in this exercise that confirmed your own view of yourself? (What was not a surprise?)

_____

_____

_____

_____

_____

_____

_____

_____

_____

_____

2. What surprised you about yourself in doing this exercise?

_____

_____

_____

_____

_____

_____

_____

_____

_____

_____

_____

3. Has your Mystery window pane become smaller or larger? How? Why?

_____

_____

_____

_____

_____

_____

_____

_____

_____

_____

_____

_____

_____

_____

_____

_____

Suggested Activity 2

YOUR PERSONAL PROS AND CONS FOR TEACHING

The next step in our set of self-observation activities will give you the chance, first, to compare your reasons for going into teaching with a list of reasons that in-service teachers have identified and, second, to examine and comment on a set of reasons that explains why some people do not go into teaching or end their careers rather quickly.

DIRECTIONS

1. First read each list carefully. In the first column, rate the reasons in List 1 from 1 through 6 to explain why you are going into teaching. Give the strongest reason a rating of 1, the next strongest a rating of 2, and so on. Then do the same with List 2, but this time rate only the reasons that have personal meaning to you. Give the strongest reason a rating of 1 and so on.

LIST 1 (THE REASONS WHY PEOPLE ENTER TEACHING)

_____ Enjoy working with students.

_____ Good fringe benefits (health insurance, long vacations, etc.).

_____ Doing important and honorable work.

_____ Geographic flexibility.

_____ Chance to work with people who share my goals.

_____ Preferable to options in the business world.

_____ Job stability.

_____ Doing something good for the community.

_____ Daily/yearly schedule that gives me time to myself.

_____ Pleasant surroundings and working conditions.

LIST 2 (THE REASONS WHY PEOPLE DO NOT GO INTO TEACHING OR LEAVE EARLY)

_____ Personally did not enjoy school and do not want to be part of it.

_____ Looking for more material rewards from work than can be gained from teaching.

_____ Do not want to be a disciplinarian.

_____ As a teacher, not enough say in educational issues and conditions of work.

_____ As a teacher, not enough opportunities for personal growth.

_____ Too much "out-of-school work" (e.g., preparations and paper corrections).

2. What does your set of ratings tell you about your reasons for going into teaching? Did your ratings in any way surprise you? If so, please explain why.

_____

_____

_____

_____

_____

_____

_____

_____

3. Read the second list of reasons and comment on how you think these factors may or may not influence your decision to begin and maintain a career in teaching. Explain why these particular reasons are meaningful or not meaningful to you.

_____

_____

_____

_____

_____

_____

_____

_____

_____

_____

_____

Suggested Activity 3

YOUR IDEAL SCHOOL

As a result of many years of schooling, and more recently as a result of your field observations, you have developed a set of standards about schools. Whether you are aware of this or not, you have an ideal school in your mind. Much of what you think about yourself and education is wrapped up in that ideal. The following questions will help you learn about and identify factors of your ideal school. By responding to each of the questions, you will reveal dimensions of your ideal *and* of yourself.

1. What is the setting for your ideal school? Rural? Suburban? Inner city? In what part of the country or state? Be as explicit as possible:

_____

_____

_____

_____

2. What is the grade level of this school? What are the students like?

_____

_____

_____

_____

3. What is your classroom like? Physically (draw it if that helps)? Psychologically? What is the emotional tone of your classroom?

_____

_____

_____

_____

4. Describe the building (age, design, furnishings, and outstanding features):

_____

_____

_____

_____

5. What other adults (if any) are part of your classroom?

_____

_____

_____

_____

_____

6. What kinds of relationships exist among the faculty members? Between you and your supervisor? How much supervision do you want?

_____

_____

_____

_____

_____

7. What are some of the things that you want to have happen in your ideal school?

_____

_____

_____

_____

_____

8. What do your answers reveal about you and your career aspirations?

_____

_____

_____

_____

_____

_____

Suggested Activity 4

SETTING PERFORMANCE PRIORITIES

"The good teacher" is a practical idea, but it is also an ideal. As elementary and secondary school students, we trudged off to school each September, hoping that this year would be different, that this year we would get "the good teacher," the one who would like us and teach us to like school. Sometimes we came close to the ideal, but usually not.

There is, of course, no ideal teacher. Nor is one set of characteristics or competencies ideal for all teaching situations. However, there has been a substantial amount of exhortation, debate, and research in this area in recent years. The competency- or performance-based movement in teacher education, which gained momentum during the 1970s, is a result of all this ferment, and it has produced several useful lists of important teacher competencies. For example, as a result of an extensive study at Iowa State University, Dick Mannette (1984) and his associates came up with a thorough list of teacher competencies. These competencies, or performance areas, are based on teaching effectiveness research as well as on the practical desires of principals, school boards, and superintendents.

These competencies—or criteria, as they are called in Mannette's assessment instrument—were distributed into four major performance categories: productive teaching techniques, classroom management, positive interpersonal relations, and professional responsibilities. You will recognize many of the performance areas, or competencies, listed next as the "basic stuff" of teaching, and it is almost certain that you will be evaluated in terms of *some* of these criteria if you choose to become a teacher. Therefore, it will be useful now, as you consider your decision to become a teacher and move beyond that to consider a plan for personal growth in teaching, for you to read through the list that follows and (1) put a check (√) next to the performance areas in which you believe you currently possess some skill or strength and (2) put a plus sign (+) next to the areas in which you believe you have a lot to learn (high-growth areas).*

In some of the performance areas, particularly Performance Category 4, you may find it difficult to rate yourself. *You do not need to put a √ or a + next to each of the twenty-six performance areas to complete this activity*. Actually, rating yourself in even half of these performance areas will be a positive step toward completing the final and most important activity in this chapter.

---

*The list employed in this text is the authors' revision of materials presented in the previously cited document coauthored by Richard Mannette.

Student Name: _____ Date: _____

PERFORMANCE CATEGORY 1 (PRODUCTIVE TEACHING TECHNIQUES)	Strength Area	High-Growth Area

The teacher is able to

1. Demonstrate effective lesson-planning skills. _____ _____

2. Demonstrate effective lesson-sequence and unit-planning skills. _____ _____

3. Effectively implement lesson plans. _____ _____

4. Motivate students. _____ _____

5. Effectively communicate with students. _____ _____

6. Effectively diagnose students. _____ _____

7. Provide students with specific evaluative feedback. _____ _____

8. Display a thorough knowledge of subject matter. _____ _____

9. Set appropriate expectations for student achievement. _____ _____

10. Provide learning opportunities for individual/idiosyncratic learners. _____ _____

11. Effectively manage classroom learning time. _____ _____

12. Select and effectively teach content that is congruent with the prescribed curriculum. _____ _____

Student Name: _____ Date: _____

	Strength Area	High-Growth Area
PERFORMANCE CATEGORY 2 (CLASSROOM MANAGEMENT)		
The teacher is able to		
13. Make effective use of time, materials, and human resources.	_____	_____
14. Demonstrate evidence of personal organization.	_____	_____
15. Set appropriate standards for student behavior.	_____	_____
16. Organize students for effective instruction.	_____	_____
PERFORMANCE CATEGORY 3 (POSITIVE INTERPERSONAL RELATIONS)		
The teacher is able to		
17. Demonstrate effective interpersonal relationships with others.	_____	_____
18. Demonstrate awareness of the needs of students.	_____	_____
19. Promote positive self-concept(s).	_____	_____
20. Demonstrate sensitivity in relating to students.	_____	_____
21. Promote self-discipline and responsibility.	_____	_____
PERFORMANCE CATEGORY 4 (PROFESSIONAL RESPONSIBILITIES)		
The teacher is able to		
22. Demonstrate employee responsibilities.	_____	_____
23. Support school regulations and policies.	_____	_____
24. Assume responsibilities outside the classroom as they relate to school.	_____	_____
25. Engage in professional self-evaluation.	_____	_____
26. Respond positively to suggested improvements in a timely manner.	_____	_____

Student Name: _____ Date: _____

Journal Entry

Because this is the final chapter in this workbook and because a major objective of this workbook was to place you into a position to make a more informed choice about entering, or not entering, the teaching profession, it would be appropriate in this final Journal Entry for you to

1. Share your decision.
2. Explain why you have made this decision.
3. Discuss how the journey that this workbook led you through contributed to your decision or the reasons for your decision.

_____

_____

_____

_____

_____

_____

_____

_____

_____

_____

_____

_____

_____

_____

_____

_____

_____

Questions for Discussion

1. Which two activities in this workbook were most illuminating for you? Why?
2. Which of your five specific objectives are you going to "work" on first?
3. Did the rating and self-analysis activities in this chapter lead you to specify, in your final five objectives, objectives that were a surprise to you?
4. If you had been asked to produce a set of five "growth" objectives at the beginning of the course, which of the final five that you produced would likely not have been included?

References

Dewey, J. (1938). *Experience and education.* New York: Macmillan.

Luft, J. (1970). *Group processes: An introduction to group dynamics* (2nd ed.). Palo Alto, CA: National Press.

Mannette, R., and Stow, S. B. (1984). *Clinical manual for teacher performance evaluation.* Ames, IA: Iowa State University Foundation.

Tripp, D. (1993). *Critical incidents in teaching: Developing professional judgment.* New York: Routledge.

INDEX

TO THE OWNER OF THIS BOOK:

I hope that you have found *Lenses on Teaching, Developing Perspectives on Classroom Life*, Fourth Edition useful. So that this book can be improved in a future edition, would you take the time to complete this sheet and return it? Thank you.

School and address:_____

Department:_____

Instructor's name:_____

1. What I like most about this book is:_____

_____

_____

2. What I like least about this book is:

_____

_____

3. My general reaction to this book is:

_____

_____

4. The name of the course in which I used this book is:

_____

5. Were all of the chapters of the book assigned for you to read?_____

   If not, which ones weren't?_____

6. In the space below, or on a separate sheet of paper, please write specific suggestions for improving this book and anything else you'd care to share about your experience in using this book.

_____

_____

_____

_____

THOMSON

WADSWORTH

BUSINESS REPLY MAIL
FIRST-CLASS MAIL   PERMIT NO. 34   BELMONT CA

POSTAGE WILL BE PAID BY ADDRESSEE

Attn: *Dan Alpert, Education Editor*
Wadsworth/Thomson Learning
10 Davis Dr
Belmont CA 94002-9801

OPTIONAL:

Your name: _____ Date: _____

May we quote you, either in promotion for *Lenses on Teaching, Developing Perspectives on Classroom Life*, Fourth Edition, or in future publishing ventures?

Yes: _____   No: _____

Sincerely yours,

Leigh Chiarelott

Leonard Davidman

Kevin Ryan